Moreton Morrell Site

£15.00
712.
23)

CHANGING
GARDENS

First published in Great Britain in 2001 by Hamlyn,
an imprint of Octopus Publishing Group Limited,
2–4 Heron Quays, London, E14 4JP

Distributed in the United States and Canada by
Sterling Publishing Co., Inc.
387 Park Avenue South, New York, NY 10016–8810

ISBN 0 600 60202 8

A catalogue record for this book is available from the
British Library

Printed in China

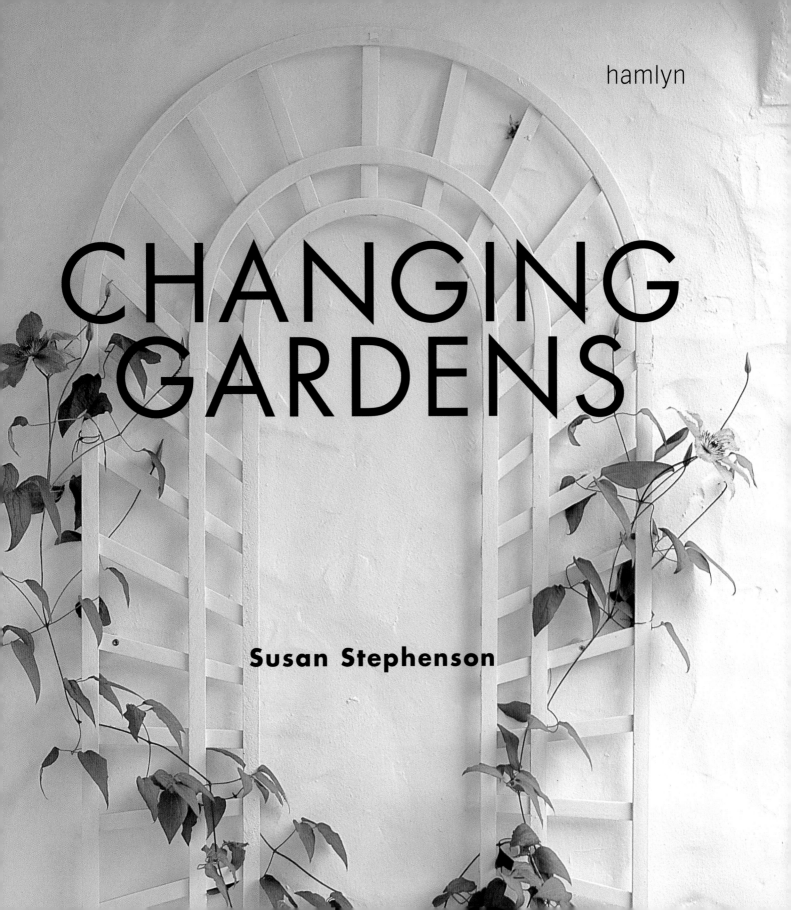

CHANGING GARDENS

Susan Stephenson

hamlyn

CONTENTS

INTRODUCTION

A well planned and well maintained garden can be a source of pleasure all year round, when you are on the patio enjoying the scents of favourite roses on a warm summer's evening or when you catch a glimpse of delicate snowdrops in winter.

Whether you are contemplating changing your existing garden or have instead moved into a new house which has only the bare beginnings of garden, take the time to assess your plot, looking at its good and bad points and thinking about what you want from your personal space. Only when you are sure that the garden of your dreams will be the garden that suits your pocket and your lifestyle should you begin to turn your dreams into reality.

The essence of good garden design lies in creating an area that is visually pleasing but that also fits in with your needs. The first part of this book looks at the aspects you will need to consider when planning your garden. There is practical advice on a variety of garden questions from the common problem of dealing with a sloping plot to deciding where to position garden ornaments. Deciding what style of garden you'd like is also discussed. Is a sophisticated roof terrace designed for outside entertaining right for you or do you need space for a greenhouse or for children to play?

Once you have decided what sort of garden you'd like, move on to the second part of the book. Here are 20 original designs, together with detailed planting plans. From a formal pool garden to one designed to encourage wildlife these designs can be to copied, adapted or simply used for inspiration for your dream garden.

DESIGNING YOUR GARDEN

Do not be deterred from designing your own garden by any preconceived ideas that it is a complicated process that has to be entrusted to highly paid designers and professional builders. Provided you are aware of your own limitations and the limitations that will be imposed by the site, the processes of planning and creating a garden are within the capabilities of most gardeners.

Begin by asking yourself what you want from your garden. Are you a keen plant collector? Do you have small children? Do you want vegetables or cut flowers? Assess your site and consider what is possible and what will be impossible. If, for example, you have a shady garden, there will be little point in a design that incorporates large flowerbeds filled with sun-loving plants. Similarly, if you live in an area of chalky soil, there will be some plants that will never thrive in your garden.

Next, work out how much you can afford to spend on your new garden. There is no point in thinking up a grand scheme if you cannot afford to carry it out. Then, work out how much spare time you have to spend in the garden in order to maintain it. If you lead a hectic life you may well not have a lot of time for your garden, in which case you should think about working out a low-maintenance scheme.

When you have looked at all the practicalities, start thinking in more detail. Do you want grass or paving? How much border space do you think you will need? More to the point, perhaps, how much time will you have to keep your borders looking good? On the whole, paving is easier to maintain than grass, which must be mowed regularly. Borders, even when filled with shrubs, need a certain amount of work to keep them looking their best.

When you have roughly divided the garden into areas of paving, grass and borders, or a combination of any two, make a list of features you want. Go into the garden with a notebook and look around. Jot down ideas that come to you, then go indoors again to imagine what your new garden will look like from both downstairs and upstairs windows.

If your garden is a difficult shape – perhaps it is short and wide, or long and thin – try to work out how to disguise this. Remember that a garden will appear longer than it is if you have a diagonal layout that leads the eye from a front corner to an opposite back corner. If you want to make your garden seem shorter, divide it into separate compartments or 'rooms', which can be linked by a winding path.

Don't be discouraged by sloping ground. A contoured garden is, in fact, usually more interesting than a perfectly flat one, so make the most of slopes by including a waterfall or rock garden in your plans, and if it is very steep you can make a series of terraces and raised beds.

Once you have decided on your new design and drawn it on your plan, you may need to get professional help with any major work, such as moving large amounts of soil, or with the hard landscaping. Do not try to do everything yourself if you do not have the expertise to do so. In the long run it is much more time- and cost-effective to get professional help.

On the following pages we look more closely at the various factors you need to consider before you can commit your ideas to paper. No two gardens are the same, and no two gardeners want the same things from their gardens, but it is worth taking all the following aspects into account in a methodical way rather than approaching the design process piecemeal.

Assessing the Site

The most important part of deciding how to make a new garden or how to improve an existing one is to understand your area, for the character of a garden is influenced by climatic conditions, soil, aspect, views (or the lack of them), the buildings around you and so on. The combination of these disparate factors may seem so unpromising as to be difficult, but no site is incapable of being improved by thoughtful design and carefully chosen plants.

Whether your site is brand new or an old, established plot, the same principles apply to planning and designing your garden. First, assess what you have got, then decide what kind of garden you want and whether you can achieve it. Assess your garden's potential, its strengths and weaknesses, and identify the ways in which you can take advantage of all

that is good about it and play down the bad points. But, remember: nothing happens overnight, and you will not wake up the next morning to find the perfect garden.

CLIMATE AND MICROCLIMATE

Climate is all-important because it dictates the kinds of plant you can grow, and this will influence your design. If you have moved to a new area it is easy to discover average temperatures and rainfall, but you must always allow for extremes.

Regional climate is influenced by fundamental geographical factors such as the latitude, the altitude, the proximity of large land masses and the sea and the influence of major ocean currents. Some districts also have their own local weather patterns such as seasonal winds.

Then there are microclimates, natural and artificial. Most cities, for example, are nearly frost-free because of the artificial heat exuded by buildings. Consequently, many tender plants can be kept outside in towns that in colder country areas would have to be protected over winter.

Although it is necessary to learn about your local climate, it is equally important to set about creating your own microclimate. You cannot do much about the weather, but you can do a great deal to minimize its effects, perhaps by putting up a protective windbreak against icy winds, which will allow you to grow a wider range of delicate and more interesting plants. In cold areas, frost and snow will do no harm provided you grow hardy plants and do not leave tender perennials outside without any protection.

SOIL TYPES

The better the quality of the soil that you have in your garden, the better your plants will grow. If your soil is poor and infertile you will find it necessary to improve it, but first, because soils vary hugely in texture, structure and quality, you need to begin by working out exactly what type of soil you have in the garden.

Most people need know only whether the soil in their garden is clayey or sandy, because this will influence your choice of plants. Clay retains moisture, but it is difficult to work and sticky when wet and it sets very hard with surface cracks in a dry summer. It needs regular breaking up over winter with a soil conditioner, although it is often very fertile in its own right. Sandy soil is easy to work and dries out quickly, but needs plenty of well-rotted manure or compost to improve moisture retention. Alluvial silt in a flood plain is an exception to the sandy rule; it is easy to work, fertile and, although free-draining, excellent at retaining moisture.

ACIDITY AND ALKALINITY

Before you begin to select plants, you should also know the character of your soil – that is, whether it is acid or alkaline. If it is alkaline you will not be able to grow lime-hating plants such as rhododendrons and camellias. On the other hand, plants that prefer limy soil, such as philadelphus, clematis and dianthus, will not thrive in very acid soils.

It is worth buying one of the inexpensive soil-testing kits to discover the pH of your garden. Test soil from different parts of the garden because conditions can vary within even fairly small areas. To confirm your readings do a little reconnaissance: talk to people, ask local gardeners for their advice and opinions, and look around the neighbourhood to see what plants are growing well in other people's gardens. If you want to increase the alkalinity of your soil add lime, but think carefully before you do this because it is long lasting. It is not as easy to increase the acidity. The best way is to create raised beds, or special enclosures, which can be filled with acid soil for ericaceous plants.

opposite: Tall trees, high yew hedges and low box edging create a sheltered microclimate for the abundance of plants in these double borders.

left: A paved town garden offers the opportunity to use containers and create beds filled with soils exactly suited to the needs of the plants you want to grow.

left: This large paved patio is positioned in a sunny part of the garden, while tall trees shade the summerhouse to create a cool retreat on scorching summer days.

opposite: Full use has been made of this white-themed corner, with a raised bed packed full of flowers and simple painted trellis to support climbers and wall shrubs.

SUN, SHADE AND SHELTER

The quality of light will have a major influence on your garden design. Shade is usually more of a problem in towns than in the countryside, because next-door buildings and neighbouring walls and fences tend to cast shadows for at least part of the day. If only a corner of your garden receives sun, for example, it makes sense to reserve this area for a garden bench, patio or greenhouse. Do not waste the sun you do have.

Shelter is another factor to consider in the planning process. For the best possible results, plants need a sheltered site, and the ideal garden is one that provides an enclosed haven in which they can thrive. Wind can be a major problem because it dehydrates the soil and stunts plant growth. If your site is badly exposed the first thing you should do is build some kind of windbreak. Although it may seem a good idea to build a solid wall, this does more harm than good because the wind will eddy over the top of the wall and swirl down, creating a whirlwind effect in your garden. A filtering windbreak, such as an open-work fence or a hedge, is far better for your plants.

Protecting your plants from frost is as important as protecting them from cold, drying winds. In winter frost is seldom a problem, given that there are more than 60,000 hardy plants to choose from, and it is possible to choose plants to suit most tastes in even the coldest areas. Frost at the wrong time of year, on the other hand, will kill plant growth. In valleys or ground hollows you may well get what is known as a 'frost pocket'. This is when cold, frosty air sinks to the lowest part of the landscape and collects beneath walls or closely planted hedges. Frost will also collect under a thick hedge or solid wall. If you thin or remove trees or walls, you will let the cold air flow through your garden rather than trapping it within it.

DIMENSIONS

In order to make the most of your space, you will have to familiarize yourself with its dimensions. Size matters, but only in so far as it might limit the number of different areas you can create and the size and number of plants and features within them.

If your garden is small there are several ways of putting the available space to more efficient use: vertical surfaces, for instance, offer scope for climbers, wall plants and hanging baskets. Raised beds and terraces extend the growing areas, and containers make maximum use of paved areas.

Although most gardeners find themselves with too little space rather than too much, having too much space can be a problem. In this case, strategic planting, with the emphasis on trees and shrubs underplanted with ground cover, will help to make the garden seem smaller and more intimate.

SHAPE

Your garden design will be greatly influenced by the shape of the plot. Few gardens are perfectly symmetrical, but that really does not matter. An L-shape or a triangle can even offer more design potential than a rectangle, and perhaps the most difficult shape of all is a square, particularly when it is too small to subdivide, as is the case with many suburban front gardens.

A design for an awkward shape needs to be carefully thought out. A long, narrow area, for example, can be divided into contrasting sections with barriers across its width, but if you break up the barriers so that it is just possible to see from one end of the garden to the other you create an additional sightline. In addition, placing an ornamental feature, such as a statue or seat, at the far end will enable you to gain the full benefit from the site's length, while the screens minimize the disadvantages of its shape.

TOPOGRAPHY

Think twice before you begin to level any slopes in your garden. Surprisingly perhaps, a level site offers less potential for an exciting design than one with interesting, gradual changes. Slopes, banks and changes of level all offer opportunities for building terraces, retaining walls or stepped beds, or for a feature such as a raised pool or rock garden.

DIVISION

Hedges, walls and fences make ideal screens and can introduce different moods and styles as you walk through the garden. They are also invaluable for screening off unattractive but necessary areas, such as the compost heap and refuse storage areas. Do not simply erect screens and forget about them: they ought to be attractive, architectural features.

ATMOSPHERE

The mood of your garden is an important consideration. Even when you are working on a bare site, the potential of the space needs to be assessed and compared with the 'feel' you want to achieve. Walk around the area, take measurements and observe natural features. When you are preparing the plan, the emphasis should be on making use of the natural resources and converting apparently insignificant areas of the garden into eye-catching attractions.

WHAT YOU WANT FROM YOUR GARDEN

Having assessed the physical advantages and disadvantages of the site, next examine your own particular needs. What do you want from the garden as a space and as an extension of your lifestyle? Do you want somewhere where you will be able to rest and relax, somewhere to entertain your friends and enjoy a barbecue, or somewhere for your children to play? Are you interested in the possibilities of attracting wildlife into your garden, or do you want to build up a specialist collection of plants? Do you want somewhere to grow your own fruit and vegetables?

In a large garden the problem of having to decide on your priorities does not arise; your concern will be how much space to assign to each area and how to divide the one from the other. In a smaller plot, however, you will have to limit yourself to one or perhaps two areas. The less space there is to play with, the more ingenious the design must be.

LINKING HOUSE AND GARDEN

When you are indoors, the view through the windows into your garden is at least as important as the view from any vantage point outside. Your garden design must, therefore, include views that look tempting from inside, from the rooms where you spend most time. If you are lucky enough to look out over open countryside or a fine cityscape, make sure the garden design blends with the background. A cottage garden-style design is much more suitable for a rural area than a modern design, while the latter will look more appropriate in an urban setting.

Conversely, when you are in the garden and look back towards the house, the building should be an integral part of the design. A conservatory or sun room can be designed to open on to a terrace or patio so that in summer, when the doors are open, the garden feels as if it is extending into the house and vice versa. Climbers and wall plants help soften the harsh outline of a building and act as a link between the house and the garden.

ESTABLISHED FEATURES

In many ways, when you are planning a garden it is easiest to begin with a bare site, because you can do more or less what you like with it, providing there are no overwhelming restrictions, such as planning regulations or covenants, on the land.

It is far more difficult to rework an established garden. Before you demolish the existing features or dig up any of the plants, however, wait one full season. This delay is essential. Even an apparently hideous layout is likely to have some redeeming feature that will be worth preserving, although it may not be immediately obvious.

Note the presence of any existing spring bulbs, shrubs that provide winter interest with colourful stems or graceful outlines and any plants with unusual autumn seedheads. Identify boggy, waterlogged areas and any parts of the garden that appear to dry out quickly. Are these features that you might like to keep?

Obvious features, such as large trees or natural water courses, can cause problems. How will they look when they are incorporated into a new design? It is impossible to suggest general solutions, but consider the following. If the tree or natural feature is particularly fine, rare or special in any other way, would it be possible to reshape your design to work around the feature? Because maturity will be lacking in a new garden and because achieving an established appearance will be one of your aims, is it possible to keep the feature in the medium term until the garden has mellowed and matured and then think about replacing it with your ideal specimen tree or sculpture?

Hard landscaping and architectural and ornamental features present less of a problem than natural features because in most cases they can be dismantled and relocated. The advantage of re-using such existing materials – stone walls and troughs, paving slabs, millstones and so on – is that they will already be weathered and worn, unlike the rather sterile appearance of new materials.

TIME AND MONEY

Time and money are two major factors to take into consideration when you are designing your garden. Only plan a garden that you can afford to make – and, incidentally, that you can comfortably afford to maintain – within a realistic timescale.

The joy of gardening is that it suits every pocket. Landscaping a small area with choice materials and lavish, mature plants can be

expensive; using inexpensive materials, propagating as many plants as possible and being prepared to wait while plants become established is the best way to develop a fine garden on a tight budget.

Interim measures have their uses. Fill beds with annuals until you can afford more expensive shrubs or until the perennials have grown to their full potential and fill their allocated space. An arrangement of attractive pots will provide a focal point until a statue or sculpture has been added.

STARTING THE DESIGN

Once you know all about your site, exactly what you want from your garden, what inherited features are worth preserving and how much time you want to spend on maintenance, you can begin the design.

To generate some useful ideas, stand in the garden – or on the patch of wasteland that is to become your garden – and think in terms of shapes and colours. As ideas begin

to form, you can explore practicalities and solve problems. At this planning stage, allow your imagination to wander and take plenty of time to consider all the options.

MARKING OUT YOUR GARDEN

The practical business of designing – preparing drawings to scale, organizing plant lists and so on – appears to be far more daunting than it really needs to be. Accuracy is important but it is not that difficult to achieve; if you are methodical and careful, the site can be carefully measured and a true plan drawn. Use graph paper so that every element is correctly in scale.

If you find it difficult to visualize designs from lines on a piece of paper, there is really no reason why you should not use the garden itself as your drawing board. The site, if not already clean, will have to be cleared of any rubbish or unwanted objects before you begin. Then, using sticks and lengths of string (preferably strong and visible baler

twine) as your pen and ink, mark out where everything should go. Keep making adjustments to these markers until you have the layout you want. A length of hosepipe is ideal for marking out areas with curved edges such as the front of a border or a natural pool.

Complicated details may need a more striking outline, which can be done with whitewash brushed over the ground. It is also worth visualizing height where this is a vital factor. A stepladder erected to the height of a mature hedge will give you a good idea of the ultimate effect. If this looks too tall, obscuring a fine view and casting too much shade, select a different hedging plant. Put a chair in a proposed seating area and try it out. Is this the best place or will it be ruined by an unattractive view? Will your proposed seat be in a sunny spot in the morning but in shade in the afternoon, when you are more likely to be relaxing in the garden?

When you have a clearer idea of the arrangement of your site it will be easier to transfer the details to paper. Although you may think you have a clear idea in your mind of what you want to achieve, a plan will be an essential point of reference once the heavy work has begun. Before you draw up the plan, however, leave the markers in place for a week or so to make sure that all the ideas are going to work in practice. Only then, when you are certain that the main elements of the design are as you really want them, should you draw up the plan.

Design Guidelines

Inevitably, personal taste is bound to govern your final design, but there are a number of basic design principles that affect every scheme. These guidelines not only help to ensure that experienced gardeners do not overlook any of the necessary planning stages along the way, but they will also help less confident gardeners to attempt more ambitious schemes and to translate their ideas successfully into reality.

FIRST STEPS

Because the garden will be viewed mostly from the house, your first action should be to go indoors and make all your major design decisions from the appropriate windows. Second, do not forget that the house is part of the garden; a garden design completely at odds with the style of your house will never look appropriate.

It is a good idea to go out and look at examples of different types of garden for inspiration before you start to make your own plans. At least then you will begin to realize that almost anything is possible.

FORMALITY AND INFORMALITY

Gardens are sometimes classified as being either formal or informal, which you might interpret as being regular and geometric or irregular and freehand. Formal gardens are mostly symmetrical, with a central path or lawn and identical (or similar) features on each side. Informal gardens tend to be pictorial rather than patterned and scarcely ever repeat the same idea. They are more likely to consist of flowing curves than straight lines or geometric shapes.

One way of designing your garden is to make the area near the house formal but gradually make the layout less formal the further away from the house you go. This formula works well because it ties the house into the garden in a gentle and subtle way, but there is nothing to stop you having a completely formal or completely informal garden, or a bit of both. A popular alternative is to create a series of 'rooms', using alternate formal and informal designs. You will end up with a garden full of variety and surprises, which will tempt visitors to wander further to find out what is around the next corner. Many gardens have an underlying formality that is masked by a mass of informal planting. This can produce the most delightful results: a sort of controlled chaos.

Before deciding which is the more visually satisfying, formality or informality, or, indeed, a mixture of the two, think about what suits you best. Formal gardens tend to rely on tidiness and precision for their impact, which means constant weeding and trimming. Informal gardens can be left to grow and are usually easier to maintain. A formal scheme is not a good idea if you have small children.

DECIDING ON THE BASIC LAYOUT

The starting point of any new design is deciding on a basic layout. Try to resist the temptation to line everything up in a series of parallel lines. Instead, explore the possibilities of creating more exciting shapes by making use of diagonals and curves.

Most gardens have a rectangular layout, a diagonal layout or a circular layout. A rectangular approach consists of symmetrical features and a lot of straight lines and predictable curves, and such a design is often more suited to a small town garden than a larger country one. The built-in angle of a diagonal layout will offset features to produce a less predictable, more relaxed and interesting effect. A curved layout is appropriate in a large, rambling garden.

SHAPE AND PATTERN

The use of different shapes and patterns is perhaps the single most important element in designing a garden. In a really good garden the shape and pattern of every component, from the broad sweep of a path or lawn to details such as the contrasting shapes of miniature shrubs in a carefully positioned stone trough, will have been thoroughly thought out.

Shapes introduce movement, balance and punctuation to a garden design. Movement can come from the repeated use of upright shapes, such as arches, which take the eye away into the distance. The effect will work either in a formal, symmetrical context or in a more informal, zigzag fashion. Balance will help the garden to look restful to the eye: a dramatic upright shape can be countered by an adjoining low mound, and the two can be held together by some horizontal shapes.

Some patterns – squares and circles within squares, for example – are static and restful because they are self-contained shapes that do not lead anywhere, whereas diagonals and curves are active and full of movement because they lead from one place to another. A static design is appropriate for a formal, regularly shaped garden, while an active design is better for an informal garden. Make sure that all the lines of your pattern lead the eye towards some focal point, which could be a specimen tree or a statue. This will create the 'pace' of the garden and link it up into a coherent and satisfying whole.

Apart from these structural uses of shape, a garden is kept alive and interesting through its detail, by the constant interplay between neighbouring plants.

opposite: In this formal design tightly clipped, zigzagged box edging encloses well-planted borders in which foliage and form predominate.

left: An informal border in which a mass of flowers and foliage intermingle happily and spill over the curved edge on to the lawn.

HORIZONTAL AND VERTICAL SURFACES

Use vertical structures – walls, fences, screens, gateways, pergolas and garden buildings – and horizontal structures – drives, paths, patios and steps – sensitively, because certain shapes and materials relate to one another while others do not. For a successful garden design you should use the vertical and horizontal together in a pleasing and harmonious way to create a unified whole. Try to achieve a balance between both planes. An arch will complement a straight pathway, for example, as will a low wall built around a patio.

CONTOURS

Not everyone is blessed with an easy, level site for a garden, but those who are often long for a more varied terrain. Whatever your preference, there is no doubt that level ground makes gardening easier and that changes of level pose a set of problems, both in planting and with access.

Steep slopes can be used for streams or waterfalls, but to maximize on planting space you can terrace the slope using either retaining walls or turf banks. Groups of Mediterranean-type plants, such as *Lavandula* spp. (lavender) and *Santolina* spp. (cotton lavender), will thrive on sunny slopes, where drainage will be quick and efficient. These are also the perfect conditions for a scree garden, which will be more interesting to look at than a single planting. Cold, shady slopes make good woodland gardens, but will equally make an ideal site for a terraced alpine garden because they are naturally well drained, fully exposed to light, but without the drying heat that is to be found on a sunny slope.

How you decide to use the contours in your garden also depends on the relationship of the slope or slopes to the house. A garden that slopes up from the house is far more dominant than one that slopes away. Sites that slope away from the house are less imposing and throw into the distance. If the view is good, and it can be relied upon to remain so, make the most of it, but if you want to keep the focus within the garden try using a formal arrangement of large pots or upright conifers. These may not mask a poor view but they will give details of some substance to attract the eye.

Irregular changes of level within a garden can make it more interesting and offer an opportunity to create surprise views and features. The move from one level to another does not necessarily have to be negotiated in one go, of course – a flight of steps can be split up and intermediate levels inserted between them. If the garden contains large mounds or hollows, consider enlarging them to create a major feature, such as a pond or rock garden.

MANIPULATING SCALE

If your garden is small or an awkward shape, you can disguise the fact by using various design devices. Most people want to increase the apparent size, or at least make a small garden seem less confined; others aim to make a broad site with little depth appear longer than it is or to make a long, narrow garden seem less tunnel-like.

Making a small garden appear less cramped is often most successful when you avoid any single, unified design, which tends only to emphasize the size of the site. If you break the space down into even smaller portions, your eye will quickly move from one part to another and focus on the details of the planting and hard landscaping rather than on the larger picture. If you give these spaces different characters, you will increase a feeling of diversity within your small site. Try to create a garden where paths wind in among the plants in such a way as never to reveal the full extent of the site.

Long, narrow gardens can also be treated in this way, so that it is never possible to see down the full length of the long axis. It also helps if you try to arrest the eye with some major feature in the foreground or middle distance, such as a circular lawn or a specimen tree, or if you place horizontal features, such as low walls, wide steps, paving or hedges, across the axis. In a less symmetrical garden, place features down the sides – perhaps a painted seat or the striking trunks of a multi-stemmed tree – so that your eye will swerve and pause.

There are many ways of increasing the sense of depth in a garden. Vistas can be emphasized and 'lengthened' by stressing the distant perspective. Eyecatching features can be used to draw the eye away into the distance, but there is no need to rely solely on the contents of your garden to do this. Make use of the landscape outside: let the outside world become the focus of your garden vista. If you are fortunate enough to have a garden with an extensive view, make the most of it. Use trees and shrubs to frame a glimpse of the scene beyond the garden.

Creating false perspective is another useful trick. If you place large plants in the foreground and small ones of the same shape in the distance, all the plants will appear to be the same size although they recede into the distance. You can do the same with foliage by planting thin, airy foliage close by and denser foliage further away. Mower stripes in a lawn can be used to give direction to a view or to pull your eye in a particular direction, lengthening or shortening the perspective.

Arches, pergolas, trellis and fences all have a strong linear impact, which can be a tremendous help when you are trying to make sightlines. Trellis can also be used for *trompe-l'oeil* effects, giving the impression of three dimensions where only two exist. There are many ways of achieving these effects. Even mirrors have been used in garden doorways to double the length of a vista. Water, too, will reflect the garden away and so give the impression of space.

opposite: The vertical lines of this ornate gazebo complement the well- defined horizontals of the paving and grass paths with their neat brick edging. The curves of its design echo the shape of the backrest on the seat beneath.

right: A stone path winds its way up a series of steps on a terraced slope, flanked by dense planting of varieties that thrive in the sunny, well-drained conditions.

Elements of Design

All gardens are made up of a mixture of three basic elements: paving, lawn and planting. Paving is a low-maintenance choice, good if you do not have a lot of time to spend actually gardening. Grass and planting are labour intensive: grass needs mowing and planting needs regular watering and weeding. Pick a combination of elements that suits your needs and how much time you have to spend in the garden.

PATIOS AND PATHS

Patios tend to look better if they are laid in symmetrical, formal designs. Wooden decking, on the other hand, is an ideal alternative for curved, flowing layouts. Decking has a much more relaxed, informal feel to it than paving. Wood is a material associated with outdoor living and leisure and, being rela-

tively soft, it is a better material than paving if you have children.

Wood generally blends with plants much better than does paving, but the texture of paving contrasts well with living material; the one is hard and solid, the other is light and full of movement. The two work well together in any garden. There are few things more attractive than the straight edge of a paved patio softened by a profusion of trailing plants.

The straight edge of paving can also be used in conjunction with curved flowerbeds and lawns within one design. The overall effect will be one of contrast: straight and curved lines, squares and circles.

Paths should be used sensitively and for a reason. A path leading nowhere will not integrate with the rest of the garden. Use curved

paths in an informal design and straight ones in a formal scheme. Rather than using a path to split the garden into two equal sections, consider running it along the shadier side of the garden instead.

LAWNS

The ideal lawn is both ornamental and practical, and there is a great deal of scope to create an individual and interesting design based on grass. Make sure the shape of the lawn harmonizes with flowerbeds, pools and other features, but you should avoid complex shapes that not only look fussy but are difficult to mow.

Most lawns are a fairly standard shape, either rectangular or square, but a gently curved lawn is a much better proposition because it gives the gardener greater freedom with which to design. A lawn flowing through your garden in this way will link up all the separate parts to make a whole.

Grass is ideal for children because it is so soft, although children and adults with sporting tastes can inflict serious damage to lawns. A sandpit area can be introduced as a temporary measure while you have a very young family; later, the space can be transformed into a raised bed or even a water feature. In a very small plot, however, it may be better to discount grass altogether and opt for a mixture of paving and borders.

ADDING THE DETAILS
Once you have decided on the framework of your garden, add the decorative details such as arches and pergolas, garden furniture, statues and other garden ornaments. Resist the temptation to have too many things, otherwise your garden will look fussy and cluttered. Whatever ornaments you are using, they should be placed so that they appear to be the inevitable outcome of the garden design, rather than just an afterthought.

INTRODUCING PLANTS
Gardens can be made wholly with plants or with artefacts, such as walls, paths, patios, steps, pools, statues and other ornaments, but the best gardens usually result from a happy blending of everything. The hard landscaping and the ornamental structures will be there all year round, will not change with the seasons and will give the garden permanent form and character. Plants, on the other hand, will be constantly changing in size and appearance, and annual and bedding plants will actually be renewed every year, or even two or three times a year. Many beautiful gardens are made by creating a firm design with the architectural components and then clothing this with a rich and diverse covering of plants.

Borders and flowerbeds can be any shape – formal and straight or gently curving – and they can be backed by a wall, fence or hedge or stand in the middle of a lawn or a gravelled area as an island bed.

opposite: This cleverly designed patio in a sheltered corner is based on three circles: one of gravel, one of paving, and the third combining the two materials. Low-growing plants and carefully placed stones soften the edges.

left: A curved lawn and grass path provide a feeling of flowing movement through a garden packed with plants.

21

GARDEN ORNAMENTS

Generally speaking, decorating your garden is a matter of personal taste, and your choice of ornament will create a garden that is unique to you. Whatever item you select, it should look good in its own right and be appropriate to the setting, either standing out as a focal point or merging with the surroundings. Choose it carefully: one well-positioned statue will look far better than several pieces dotted around at random.

There are many different ornaments to consider, including statuary and other sculptures, urns and containers, and sundials and dovecotes. Topiary, the art of carving hedges into a variety of shapes, is another type of garden decoration but is a specialized skill.

Most sculpture benefits from a backdrop, such as a hedge or wall, and it will have even greater impact if it is set against a niche. Some pieces look better raised on plinths or at the top of a flight of steps. Urns and the more decorative containers also tend to look their best when raised above ground level, standing on some kind of pedestal.

PLACING SCULPTURE

Choosing the location for a sculpture is extremely important if the work is to look effective. The best approach is to decide where within the garden you want to place an object and then to set about finding a piece that will suit that location. More often, however, something irresistible is acquired, and then has to be accommodated in an appropriate setting. Some pieces will dictate a likely location: for instance, a figure of the god Bacchus will look most effective reeling drunkenly out of the bushes, while a formal statue will be more appropriately placed in a

opposite: A classic decorative
urn, raised high on a matching
plinth and backed by a dark
hedge, provides a striking focal
point at the end of a vista
through a climber-clad arched
pergola.

above: The light greens,
yellows and oranges of the
surrounding planting contrast
perfectly with the dark cast iron
of an ornate curved bench.

sharp bend of a path or at the junction of two
paths, so that the piece can be seen from two
directions. Sited centrally at the back of an
area, it can act as a focal point, but set asym-
metrically to offset the curve of a flowerbed,
the object will create a more relaxed and
informal effect. For greater formality, doorways and stairs can be flanked by sculptures.
Sculpture can also be used as a counterpoint
to a particularly bold plant, or it can be used
to distract the eye from an unsightly feature,
such as a rubbish bin or a compost heap.

For the most dramatic impact place a
sculpture in front of a clear-cut background
so that it stands out: a smooth hedge or a wall
is ideal, as long as it is higher than the statue
itself. For the opposite effect, sculpture can
be hidden away and used to create a surprise.

GARDEN FURNITURE

Furniture is an ideal way to liven up
an expanse of paving and, as well as being
decorative, it is, of course, functional.
Garden seats can also be used as focal points,
at the end of a garden, for example, or under
an arch. They are best sited in a sunny part
of the garden that receives some shade
during the day.

There is a wide selection of garden furniture to choose from to suit your particular
needs. A simple natural wooden seat will
look informal, while an ornate wooden seat,
painted dark green or white, will look much
more formal. Wrought iron furniture is one
of the smartest types and, on the whole, it
will create more of an impact since it does
not blend into the garden surroundings in
the way that wood does. More temporary
garden furniture includes picnic-type plastic
tables and chairs and canvas deckchairs.

niche or in a more commanding position,
such as on a pedestal or balustrade.

Be careful always to choose garden sculpture that is in keeping with the architecture
of the house and general surroundings, and
with the overall atmosphere you are trying to
achieve in the garden. A small statue of a pig
or a cat, for example, which is definitely rus-
tic and informal in character, will look out of
place against the formal outline of a grand,
dignified house. Such a building calls for a
more formal treatment and demands a
grand, impressive statue that is more in keeping with its style.

The most dramatic effect can be obtained
by positioning a sculpture at the end of a
vista. Alternatively, it can be placed at the

The Look of Your Garden

Whether you have a town or country garden, it is important to plan ahead to achieve the right look and design. You should also think about how far you want to plan for a low-maintenance garden.

TOWN GARDENS

Town gardens have much to offer and provide an exciting, if challenging, opportunity to produce many interesting and original garden designs. A little forward planning and careful thought can go a long way towards overcoming any immediate problems, such as lack of direct sunlight, shadows cast from neighbouring buildings, poor soil or atmospheric pollution.

Generally speaking, you will find that town gardens are easier and cheaper to maintain than most country gardens, simply because they are usually smaller. Urban sites also tend to be more sheltered than rural ones

and may even be frost-free, so that you can grow a wide range of tender plants without having to protect them or take them into a greenhouse in winter.

Formal rather than informal designs tend to be more popular for town gardens because it is easier to incorporate surrounding party walls into a methodical, precise concept. When you are choosing a design, remember that the garden will be seen as much from the upper storeys of the house as from the lower ones, and formal designs tend to look better from above than informal ones.

Size is seen as one of the most common limitations of town gardens, but there are plenty of design options that you can use to help deceive the eye. Small plots can be made to seem larger by the use of different levels linked by steps. When it comes to floor treatments, diagonal or circular paving is space enhancing. Creating separate sections within

the overall framework of the garden is another way of disguising the limited size of the area. A series of hidden areas that are linked by a winding path can help to create the illusion of space.

Lack of light is another constraint often encountered in town gardens. For those gardens surrounded by walls, it is possible to paint one or all of the walls white to reflect any light the garden receives.

Shade cast by surrounding buildings is a common problem in town gardens, and the only option here is to select shade-tolerant plants. There are many exciting ones to choose from, however, and a careful mixture of foliage and flowering plants will bring much colour and interest. Wall plants and climbers play a vital role because they increase the surface area of the garden vertically rather than horizontally. As an added attraction, a plant-clad wall or fence will provide a degree of privacy. Containers and hanging baskets can be used to make up for poor soil in the rest of the garden.

This approach of choosing plants that positively relish the prevailing situation and making the most of the available light, water and space epitomizes town gardening.

COUNTRY COTTAGE GARDENS

There is an archetypal image of the ideal country garden: from a sleepy lane, a gate in a low wall shows a broad flagged path leading to the door of an old cottage. The path is cascaded with flowers, which also burgeon from cracks in the paving, and roses twine prolifically here and there and around the door. The important point to remember is

that such a garden is lovely to look at and that it works by giving the impression of being absolutely right in its context. In the country, fitting a garden into its scene is particularly important.

The best word to sum up the cottage garden is 'unsophisticated'. It is a style in which a random variety of plants is grown, not particularly for the subtleties of careful plant association but simply as favourites, because they are loved for their own sake or because they are useful in some way. The garden in which they grow will have a small-scale, purely functional framework, without any grand vistas or extravagant hard landscaping.

In a country cottage garden the trees should, wherever possible, be fruit trees or at

least blossom trees of some kind. Apples, pears, plums and cherries will all help to create the right atmosphere, as will nut trees, such as hazel or almond. If there is space for a large tree, a walnut would be a good choice. Try to avoid large upright conifers; evergreens such as holly or a yew will look more appropriate, and they can be clipped into shapes to add a touch of fun and formality to the garden if required.

Colourful plants, or perhaps herbs, in simple pots by the door will look right. Make the most of vegetables and fruit bushes, letting them be part of the garden design. Do not be afraid of using rows of vegetables, herbs, bedding plants or flowers for cutting, especially alongside a path. There is no need to grow only old-fashioned flowers because it is how the flowers are used and grouped that creates the cottage style, not the type they are. Choose as many scented plants as can be fitted into the space available, especially from among the many varieties of climbing rose and honeysuckle.

The overall effect should be well-tended 'disorder', a comfortable mix in which all the plants are allowed to run together. There will be plenty of weeding to do, but also a great opportunity to grow all your favourite plants in rich profusion.

opposite: A wide range of shade-tolerant plants, including ferns and a spectacular large-leaved hosta, in containers have been combined with climbers and wall shrubs to make the most of this shady basement courtyard.

left: The epitome of a country cottage garden - a profusion of scented roses, lilac and lilies mingle with bright flowers and the foliage of herbs that are both ornamental and useful.

LOW-MAINTENANCE GARDENS

The labour-free garden does not exist, but there are many ways in which such chores as weeding and tidying can be kept to a minimum. Clearly, what you get out of a garden is in proportion to what you put in, and it will never be possible to expect a plant-lover's paradise to thrive on neglect. Those who want beauty without effort are being unrealistic, but there is no need to become a slave. Any method of reducing the more trouble-some tasks to a minimum is worth pursuing.

Much work can be saved by thoughtful design. Instead of grass and borders, have paving and a few raised beds. Paving is easier to maintain than lawn, and in a small garden flagstones can look better than grass.

Gravel is a novel alternative to paving in a low-maintenance garden. It is softer than paving and flows around curves, and a selection of plants that enjoy free-draining conditions will thrive in it. But, most important,

gravel laid over a semi-porous membrane will suppress weeds. When gravel is laid over soil it helps to keep down weeds and also insulates the soil against moisture loss, so you will not have to water your plants as much as those growing in an open border.

The choice of plants and their arrangement exert an enormous influence on the amount of time needed for maintenance. The aim in an easy-care garden is to make the plants themselves do as much of the work as possible. Plant shrubs that need little pruning rather than those like large-flowered roses that require more attention.

Among herbaceous varieties, those that self-seed freely without becoming invasive are ideal in a low-maintenance garden. Ground-cover plants are perfect for filling the spaces between shrubs and give excellent weed control, provided the ground in which they are planted is completely free of perennial weeds in the first place.

PATIO AND CONTAINER GARDENS

Never let it be said that container gardens are second best to gardens in the soil. They may be labour intensive but, as a reward, they can be as rich and extravagant as your pocket and patience will allow.

Containers solve many problems for would-be gardeners. They are the answer for a paved town courtyard and a roof terrace ten storeys high, and they are an excellent solution for people who cannot bend easily to dig. They are an ideal finishing touch: a collection of windowboxes can complete a house front. Whatever the purpose, the choice of containers is enormous.

There are certain ground rules to bear in mind with container gardening. You need to consider the work involved in occasional changes of soil, potting up and repotting; most important of all, you need to consider watering. Do the containers have adequate drainage? Is there a water supply nearby? Will you be able to use liquid feeds? What will happen if you are away or on holiday?

Watering is by far the greatest chore of container gardening and it needs to be done

generously and regularly. Rain is never adequate on its own, and a downpour can fool you into thinking that the containers are wetter than they really are. Automatic irrigation is well worth considering for a large container garden.

It is important to decide whether to plant for a year-round display or to let the containers remain empty in winter. Remember that many plants that would be hardy enough in the ground may succumb to the cold when their roots are raised up in a container open to frosts. Frozen, waterlogged soil can also burst containers as it expands. Conversely, containers in sun can get very hot in summer and your choice of plants needs to be governed by this fact: it is all too easy to bake the roots of plants.

With these practical points in mind, you are free to choose from the gamut of container gardening styles. Formal courtyards can be graced with potted bay trees, cypresses, camellias or bamboos. In addition, some especially beautiful pots may look best not planted at all but simply used to form an architectural contrast. Large concrete planters can be filled with trees and shrubs, almost as if they were in the ground. Stone troughs can be planted as miniature gardens of alpines or screes, but they can equally be filled with a single carpeting plant as a piece of living sculpture.

In a cottage garden style tubs, pots and even baskets of all shapes and sizes can be clustered to form splashes of colour, by doorways or lining steps. Windowboxes and hanging baskets blend in well with this style and provide an opportunity for bold or restful incidental planting in prime locations.

opposite: Gravel not only looks good but will also reduce the need for weeding and watering, making it an excellent choice of material for a low-maintenance garden.

above: The many sizes and shapes of container used in this patio garden are unified by the material from which they are all made – terracotta – and the limited colour palette of white, silver and grey from which the plants have been selected.

GARDEN PLANS

Planning a new garden is enormous fun, and for some people it is probably the most exciting stage of all in the process of creating a new garden. This is also the time to think carefully about what you want from your garden before the hard work of building it begins.

The planning process is your opportunity to sit down, pencil in hand, and put your ideas down on paper. It is a time to let your imagination run riot. Careful, constructive planning isn't all about creative instincts, however. It also requires a very cool head. There are raw materials to be considered, lifestyles to be taken into account, practicalities to be weighed up and budgets to be calculated. Above all, there are basic decisions to be made.

If you have read the first section of this book, you will already know the kind of questions you need to ask yourself. Do you have a small garden or something rather grander? Do you want a garden that looks and feels formal or would you prefer something less geometrical, less orderly? Do you plan to spend a lot of time gardening or would you like a low-maintenance option? Do you have children who need somewhere to play or will your garden be somewhere where you can indulge a passion for growing unusual plants? Is your garden square, rectangular or L-shaped, which gives you the maximum opportunity for springing surprises? Is your garden arranged on just one level or are there two, or even more, levels to be exploited? Are you content with stone and concrete or do you hanker after something more adventurous and exotic? Only when you can answer these questions can you think about beginning to draw up a detailed plan for your garden.

On the following pages are 20 different approaches to planning a garden. Take a look at them and see not only which of the gardens illustrated most closely resembles the raw materials with which you have to work, but also which of them is most like the garden you would like to have. These plans are not blueprints, to be followed slavishly, down to the positioning of the last container. They are intended instead to be a source of inspiration from which you can select features that appeal to you to enable you to create your own, ideal garden – a garden that will suit your home and your lifestyle.

PATIO GARDEN

Simple, rectangular shapes, an unusual raised platform and bold, exciting planting in raised beds and containers disguise the limited size of this enclosed patio garden and bring it vibrantly to life.

PLANTING KEY

1 Acer palmatum 'Butterfly'
2 Euphorbia characias subsp. wulfenii 'Emmer Green'
3 Hebe rakaiensis
4 Lonicera rupicola var. syringantha (syn. L. syringantha)
5 Euonymus fortunei 'Emerald 'n' Gold'
6 Philadelphus 'Manteau d'Hermine'
7 Spiraea 'Arguta' (syn. S. x arguta 'Bridal Wreath')
8 Jasminum officinale
9 Pelargonium Fragrans Group
10 Viburnum davidii
11 Stachys byzantina 'Silver Carpet'
12 Choisya ternata 'Sundance'
13 Hedera helix 'Goldchild' (syn. H. helix 'Gold Harald')
14 Kniphofia 'Little Maid'
15 Smilacina racemosa
16 Bergenia 'Bressingham White'
17 Thymus vulgaris 'Silver Posie' (syn. T. 'Silver Posie')
18 Mentha spicata (syn. M. viridis)
19 Clematis 'Nelly Moser'
20 Symphoricarpos x doorenbosii 'White Hedge'
21 Rosmarinus officinalis
22 Rodgersia podophylla
23 Rheum 'Ace of Hearts' (syn. R. 'Ace of Spades')
24 Skimmia japonica 'Wakehurst White' (syn. S. japonica 'Fructo Albo')
25 Potentilla fruticosa 'Abbotswood'
26 Euphorbia characias subsp. wulfenii 'John Tomlinson' (syn. E. characias subsp. wulfenii Kew form)
27 Ruta graveolens 'Jackman's Blue'
28 Saxifraga x geum (syn. S. 'Hirsuta')
29 Cornus alba 'Elegantissima'
30 Hydrangea paniculata
31 Pulmonaria 'Lewis Palmer'
32 Pittosporum tobira
33 Hydrangea anomala subsp. petiolaris (syn. H. petiolaris)
34 Campanula persicifolia 'Chettle Charm'
35 Hosta fortunei var. albopicta (syn. H. 'Aureomaculata')
36 Morina longifolia
37 Fatsia japonica
38 Euryops acraeus (syn. E. evansii)
39 Osmanthus delavayi
40 Passiflora caerulea 'Constance Elliot'

41 Escallonia rubra 'Woodside' (syn. E. rubra 'Pygmaea')
42 Mahonia aquifolium
43 Heliotropium 'White Lady'
44 Actinidia kolomikta
45 Euonymus fortunei 'Silver Queen'
46 Nepeta sibirica 'Souvenir d'André Chaudron' (syn. N. 'Blue Beauty')
47 Clematis montana 'Alexander'
48 Hebe 'Hagley Park'
49 Lavandula angustifolia 'Hidcote' (syn. L. 'Hidcote Blue')
50 Tamarix parviflora (syn. T. tetrandra var. purpurea)
51 Lonicera periclymenum
52 Chrysanthemum 'Golden Chalice'

53 Festuca glauca 'Elijah Blue'
54 Lavandula angustifolia 'Munstead'
55 Phormium cookianum subsp. hookeri 'Cream Delight'
56 Thuja plicata 'Rogersii'
57 Armeria maritima
58 Tanacetum argenteum
59 Sisyrinchium striatum 'Aunt May'
60 Salvia officinalis 'Purpurascens'
61 Dianthus gratianopolitanus
62 Ophiopogon japonicus
63 Cistus x hybridus (syn. C. x corbariensis)
64 Nepeta x faassenii
65 Santolina chamaecyparissus (syn. S. incana)
66 Hebe cupressoides 'Boughton Dome'
67 Phormium 'Sundowner'
68 Cotoneaster salicifolius 'Gnom'

PATIO GARDEN

A NUMBER OF DIFFERENT ELEMENTS are used to create interest and contrast in this patio garden. The simple design, based around a small rectangle, emphasizes the symmetry of the overall area, but the shape is softened and given life by the use of plants to cover angles and the bare expanses of hard landscaping. This garden is all about boldness and the careful positioning of plants to impart atmosphere to the space.

The plants at the centre and around edges are chosen to contrast with the grey pavers, which are themselves in different shades and sizes to give the illusion of texture to the surfaces. The walls of the raised beds are built of solid bricks in the same colours as the pavers to tie the garden together.

Complemented by a selection of colourful and exciting plants, this garden is the ideal place to relax after a hard day's work, while the arrangement of features and plants so that the entire garden cannot be viewed at once from the house makes it appear larger than it really is, and will entice visitors into the garden to explore every corner. Because it is sheltered, this garden will be in use for much of the year, and because it is well planned and the planting is chosen with care, it will be a delightful private retreat and an extra room to extend the living space.

FEATURES

The central feature of the garden is a raised stone platform, and there is an additional raised bed at the far end. These create dramatic changes of level without taking up any more surface space than if they were on the ground, and they have the additional advantage of bringing the plants up to eye level. The top of the platform is paved with pale slabs, and plants, chosen for their interesting leaf shape and texture, are grown in small pockets of soil. Within the platform itself there are one or two surprises, such as the small wall and the beautiful specimen plants, which can be prominently displayed on the higher level.

The uncluttered central area around the platform gives the garden a spacious, airy feel and encourages the eye to travel outwards in all directions. In all areas of this garden the hard landscape interacts and works with the planting to give a well-organized but overall impression of softness and relaxation. Because it is a strong and effective design there is no need for additional features.

PLANTING

Some of the plants in the raised beds are scented, adding a subtle, aromatic quality and reinforcing the relaxing atmosphere. The far bed is full of lush leafy plants, including *Rodgersia podophylla* and *Fatsia japonica*, to provide a dense green boundary.

The open-weave fencing provides ample space for climbers to grow and provide a green backdrop to show off the central garden. Trellis is used on the side fences to maximize the range of plants that can be grown. Climbing plants, including *Hydrangea anomala* subsp. *petiolaris* and different forms of clematis, provide a green surround and colour during the flowering season.

The colours themselves are kept largely pale except for one or two plants, largely because these paler colours make the space appear larger, but also because the generally subdued palette makes the one or two brightly coloured plants even more eyecatching without being overpowering. The subtle green, yellow, grey and blue shades of the foliage also reflect the colours of the pavers, and in a small area such as this the subtle hues and interesting textures create a harmonious and calming impression. Character and individuality are introduced by striking specimen plants, such as *Rheum* 'Ace of Hearts' and, near the edge of the central platform, *Phormium cookianum* subsp. *hookeri* 'Cream Delight'. Herbs and small shrubs are

grown together in the raised beds to provide interesting contrasts of form and habit, and the herbs release their aromas when brushed against on a summer's evening.

The rectangular shape of the raised platform and beds could emphasize the shape of the plot, but the large, rounded plants and twining climbers soften the whole area and add a gentler character. A large pot holding a specimen acer is used to add greenery to the

otherwise bare wall under the window, and trailing plants hide the edges of the raised bed to minimize the impact of the hard lines.

A few large, movable containers are used because many small containers make the garden more labour intensive. The advantage of containers is that you can grow favourite plants, moving them to get the best light and shelter. Containers can be decorated with your own designs for individuality.

opposite: This shady raised bed looks good planted with varieties in pale, gentle colours. A container-grown *Astelia chathamica* 'Silver Spear' provides a dramatic centrepiece.

above left: The leaves of the climber *Actinidia kolomikta* are strikingly variegated, yet the colours remain subdued.

above: Growing plants in the cracks between paving makes the most of every bit of planting space available, at the same time softening the lines of the hard landscaping.

TIPS FOR PATIOS

- Make sure paving stones are non-slip and are kept free from moss
- Lay paving stones on a solid base of hardcore and bed them on a cement-sand mortar, especially in areas frequently used
- Point between paving stones where plants are not required to prevent weeds from appearing
- Keep the shape of the paved areas simple and uncluttered
- Replace paving stones with decking for a warmer feel or for a softer surface if children are present
- To change the character of the garden, paint the walls of the raised beds in pretty colours
- Choose small to medium plants except for dramatic effect in one or two deep corners
- Select plants that flower in succession so there will be continuous colour
- Use lots of evergreens around the walls to give year-round cover

LOW-MAINTENANCE GARDEN

A large area of paving, the clever use of shapes and materials, and restrained yet interesting planting combine to create a low-maintenance garden that provides a haven in which to relax and looks good all year round.

PLANTING KEY

1 *Petunia* Primetime Series
2 *Pelargonium* 'Tip Top Duet'
3 *Lobelia erinus* Cascade Series
4 *Hyacinthus orientalis* 'Distinction'
5 *Tulipa biflora*
6 *Acer palmatum* 'Butterfly'
7 *Salvia patens* 'Cambridge Blue'
8 *Hebe* x *franciscana*
9 *Potentilla fruticosa* 'Elizabeth' (syn. *P. fruticosa* var. *arbuscula*)
10 *Daphne cneorum*
11 *Cistus* x *hybridus* (syn. *C.* x *corbariensis*)
12 *Pyracantha coccinea* 'Lalandei'
13 *Potentilla fruticosa* 'Sunset'
14 *Hebe albicans*
15 *Viburnum tinus* 'Pink Prelude'
16 *Lonicera fragrantissima*
17 *Phlomis* 'Edward Bowles'
18 *Hypericum bellum*
19 *Lonicera periclymenum* 'Serotina'
20 *Rosmarinus officinalis*
21 *Philadelphus* 'Belle Etoile'
22 *Olearia* x *haastii*
23 *Hebe* 'Pewter Dome' (syn. *H. albicans* 'Pewter Dome')
24 *Hydrangea involucrata* 'Hortensis'
25 *Euonymus japonicus* 'Aureus' (syn. *E. japonicus* 'Aureopictus')
26 *Osmunda regalis*
27 *Skimmia japonica* 'Veitchii' (syn. *S. japonica* 'Foremanii')
28 *Furcraea foetida* var. *mediopicta*
29 *Hosta fortunei* var. *albopicta* (syn. *H.* 'Aureomaculata')
30 *Clematis montana*
31 *Spiraea japonica* 'Anthony Waterer'
32 *Jasminum officinale*
33 *Caltha palustris*
34 *Phyllostachys flexuosa*
35 *Lobelia cardinalis*
36 *Arbutus unedo* 'Elfin King'
37 *Deutzia* x *elegantissima*
38 *Myosotis sylvatica* 'Music'
39 *Pachysandra terminalis*
40 *Platycodon grandiflorus* 'Perlmutterschale'
41 *Campanula alliariifolia*
42 *Hedera helix* 'Dragon Claw'
43 *Mahonia aquifolium*
44 *Aucuba japonica* 'Picturata'

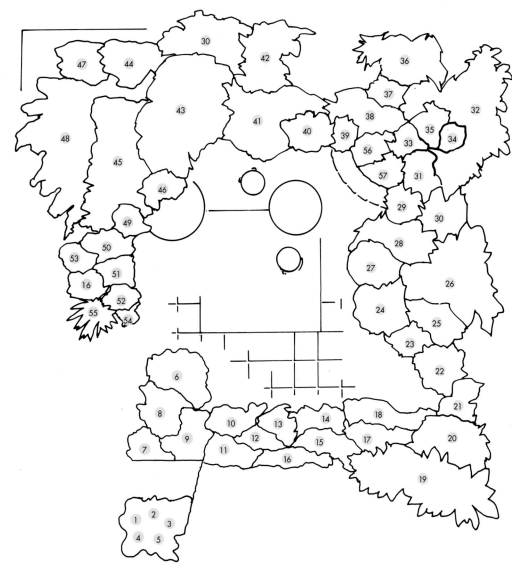

45 *Washingtonia filifera*
46 *Ailanthus altissima*
47 *Pieris japonica* 'White Cascade'
48 *Spiraea* 'Arguta' (syn. *S.* x *arguta* 'Bridal Wreath')
49 *Cytisus* x *praecox*
50 *Elaeagnus pungens*
51 *Mentha spicata* (syn. *M. viridis*)
52 *Stachys byzantina* (syn. *S. lanata*)
53 *Jasminum nudiflorum*
54 *Salvia microphylla*

55 *Cordyline fruticosa* 'Baby Ti'
56 *Pontederia cordata*
57 *Nymphaea* 'Odorata Sulphurea Grandiflora'

THE FOCUS OF THIS SIMPLE DESIGN is a relatively clear area in the centre of the garden, and there are two main features of interest, the circular seat and the raised pool. Everything has been chosen to last and to stay looking good with minimum maintenance. The brick wall at the rear of the garden, for example, is well built and will be maintenance free for many years. The design is deliberately restrained because a simple design is easier to maintain than a more complex layout covering the same area, and the simplicity of the overall scheme adds to the attraction of this garden.

The square shape of the garden has been broken up by the use of asymmetrical beds, which incorporate curves and straight lines to make the boundaries interesting and exciting. The central area is paved, because this is far easier to maintain than a lawn, and it has been left deliberately uncluttered to make the area seem larger than it actually is. A small entrance to allow access to the garden from the steps is also kept clear, but otherwise planting completely surrounds this garden to create a secluded, intimate space.

The changes in level and texture and the working contrasts between the hard landscaping and the planting make this garden feel harmonious and welcoming, the ideal place to come home to and relax.

FEATURES

The raised beds around the edges and the raised pool introduce valuable changes in height, which also serve to emphasize the central paved area. A narrow bed against the end wall unites the two sides of the garden and softens the wall. The circular tree seat in the shade of the *Ailanthus altissima* (tree of heaven) and the curved edge of the pool complement and contrast with the uniform square paving.

In the centre of the paved area a square has been marked out using a mixture of bricks, cobbles and small slabs to create an interesting and effective ornamental pattern

that will be kept clear with just the occasional sweep with a broom. Different patterns and combinations of materials – wood, brick, pebbles and gravel – could be used to create an individual pattern. This detail and the white-painted cast iron furniture in the middle of the garden, which matches the seat under the tree, draw the eye away from the boundaries and help keep attention within the garden.

The pool adds a contrast in texture and allows a greater range of plants to be grown. The smooth surface of the water reflects the foliage of the plants behind it, and additional interest is provided by the aquatics themselves, which are grown in containers in the water to prevent them from spreading into the pool and to minimize the maintenance required. The area at the rear of the pool is covered in creeping foliage to give the illusion that the pool disappears into the green-

ery behind. An alternative to the pool would be a raised bed, filled with colourful annuals, which would make a strong statement like the pool but would require more attention to keep the plants in good condition.

PLANTING

Plants have been chosen that have long seasons of interest. Some produce flowers, some bear berries, and some have autumn colours and even coloured barks in winter. In one corner is an unusual fern, *Washingtonia filifera* (desert fan palm), which will be a real focal plant and talking point, and on the opposite wall it is balanced by the smaller, but hardier, *Osmunda regalis* (royal fern).

Shrubs are used in the corners and larger beds to keep maintenance to a minimum, because once they are established they will largely take care of themselves. They create a deep, lush backdrop and a strong green backbone to the rest of the planting. Plants with strong forms, such as *Cordyline fruticosa* 'Baby Ti', are included among the softer elements of the planting to add contrast of shape and texture.

Climbers, including the fragrant *Jasminum officinale* (jasmine), grow up and along the trellis to create a light but well-defined division and provide privacy. The white bricks of the house wall reflect light into the garden and act as an effective foil to the climbing plants and wall shrubs.

Containers are used on the steps to bring the planting nearer the house. These are filled with seasonal or evergreen trailing plants. Using containers that are attractive and in complementary colours means that the garden will still have interest while the plants are dormant.

The perimeter beds vary in depth, providing great scope for a range of plants. An ingenious touch in this garden is that planting is through a porous mulching fabric, which is secured to the soil with staples of heavy-gauge fencing wire. This fabric is concealed with a mulch of bark. Many of the plants are slow growing once they have reached maturity, and this is a simple way to reduce the amount of pruning and dividing that will be needed. An irrigation system, built into the border when it is initially planted, will save time and lead to better plant growth so that the garden will mature sooner than might otherwise be expected, and annual mulching will help both to retain moisture in the soil and keep down weeds.

TIPS FOR LOW-MAINTENANCE GARDENS

- Lay flags on a sand-cement mortar base and point all joints to prevent weeds
- Invest in good quality, durable materials for furniture and other structures because these will last longer
- Make sure that the plants are kept healthy and are not overcrowded
- Prepare the soil well so that plants establish quickly and cover the ground
- Use a high proportion of evergreens for year-round interest and foliage cover
- Underplant tall deciduous shrubs with spreading ground-cover shrubs and perennials that will like the shady, dry conditions
- Do not choose plants requiring any special care and choose ones tolerant of most soils
- Select plants to give long seasons of interest
- Do jobs like pruning and sweeping up regularly so that they do not get out of hand

opposite: A raised pool, statue and arch form the focal point of this courtyard garden. Uncluttered space and a subdued palette in plants and hard landscaping create a harmonious atmosphere.

above left: The fronds of *Osmunda regalis* are dramatic when unfurled. This fern enjoys the shady, sheltered conditions of an enclosed garden.

above: An interesting and decorative edging created from a combination of bricks and pebbles in a range of colours, shapes and sizes.

GRAVEL GARDEN

Space and light are the keys to the design of this sophisticated garden. Cream-coloured gravel flows around and between a contrasting brick-paved patio and small stone-edged lawn, each material providing a different colour and texture against which plants can be displayed.

PLANTING KEY

1 *Geranium* x *oxonianum* 'Rose Clair'
2 *Ajuga reptans* 'Catlin's Giant'
3 *Cornus alba* 'Kesselringii'
4 *Dicentra macrantha*
5 *Achillea ptarmica* 'Boule de Neige'
6 *Penstemon* 'Chester Scarlet'
7 *Aconitum anthora*
8 *Persicaria affinis* 'Superba' (syn. *P. affinis* 'Dimity')
9 *Gomphrena* 'Strawberry Fields'
10 *Helianthus annuus* 'Teddy Bear'
11 *Lilium davidii*
12 *Lathyrus odorata* Multiflora Group
13 *Phormium cookianum* subsp. *hookeri* 'Cream Delight'
14 *Brassica oleracea* 'Tokyo'
15 *Sempervivum montanum*
16 *Petunia* Duo Series 'Peppermint'
17 *Begonia* 'Pin-up'
18 *Hyacinthella glabrascens*
19 *Hieracium villosum*
20 *Sedum kamtschaticum* var. *floriferum* 'Weihenstephaner Gold'
21 *Wulfenia amherstiana*
22 *Pulsatilla vulgaris*
23 *Elaeagnus pungens* 'Variegata' (syn. *E. pungens* 'Argenteovariegata')
24 *Viburnum plicatum* f. *tomentosum*
25 *Gypsophila paniculata* 'Compacta Plena'
26 *Lonicera periclymenum* 'Serotina'
27 *Stachys byzantina* (syn. *S. lanata*)
28 *Veronica spicata* subsp. *incana*
29 *Buddleja davidii* 'White Profusion'
30 *Hebe salicifolia*
31 *Viburnum* 'Eskimo'
32 *Dianthus* 'Leslie Rennison'
33 *Campanula carpatica* f. *alba* 'Bressingham White'
34 *Veronica prostrata* 'Loddon Blue'
35 *Penstemon pinifolius* 'Mersea Yellow'
36 *Campanula carpatica* 'Chewton Joy'
37 *Achillea clavennae*
38 *Seriphidium nutans* (syn. *Artemisia nutans*)
39 *Alyssum wulfenianum*
40 *Cotoneaster simonsii*
41 *Lychnis coronaria* 'Alba'
42 *Trachycarpus fortunei*
43 *Deutzia* x *elegantissima* 'Rosealind'
44 *Philadelphus* 'Sybille'
45 *Lonicera periclymenum* 'Graham Thomas'

46 *Artemisia pontica*
47 *Solidago* 'Crown of Rays' (syn. *S.* 'Strahlenkrone')
48 *Freesia* 'Ballerina'
49 *Pyrus salicifolia* 'Pendula'
50 *Ampelopsis glandulosa* var. *brevipendunculata* 'Elegans'

51 *Clematis montana* var. *rubens* 'Tetrarose'
52 *Hosta* 'Blue Blush'
53 *Bergenia* x *schmidtii* (syn. *B. ciliata* x *crassifolia*)
54 *Stachys byzantina* (syn. *S. lanata*)

GRAVEL GARDEN

GRAVEL MAKES AN IDEAL GARDEN SURFACE because it drains well and stands up to a lot of wear. It is cheap, easy to lay and easy to replace, and it is extremely versatile. Gravel is a good choice for a garden that you might want to alter later on, and it is available in many sizes and colours, which can make it the ideal contrast to other materials, such as bricks and paving.

Gravel also forms an excellent light-coloured background against which plants can be displayed. It has a softer look than most surfacing materials, and the mood of the garden changes with the weather, as gravel looks very different according to whether it is wet or dry. The inclusion of a small lawn prevents the garden from appearing rather stark.

This garden includes lots of changes in colours, textures and heights, and it is a warm, bright, cheerful asset to the house. The underlying shape of the site is square, and the design is deliberately not symmetrical to offset this. The different elements are incorporated into the comparatively small space to create an intriguing and inviting garden, which is all about contrast and harmony between brick, lawn and gravel. The raised patio makes a strong statement, but it is offset perfectly by the lawn and shrubs.

FEATURES

The gravel chosen here is cream in colour and uniform in size to create a feeling of harmony and an even texture. It gives the impression of flowing around the garden, linking all the areas and tying the garden together. The corner bed, which is planted with taller shrubs to provide seclusion, is surrounded with the gravel, which appears to continue around the bed, creating the illusion that the garden goes on beyond. This also gives the impression that the entire garden cannot be seen all at once.

A small paved patio has been built out of contrasting rectangular bricks to create a distinct area. The use of strongly coloured

bricks emphasizes the shape of the patio and provides a platform to display plants in containers, which fill this area, adding colour and warmth. The narrow walls of the patio provide the perfect perch for small pots of colourful plants and raise them to eye level. A smaller square has been built in front of the patio with larger white bricks, and this houses a sunken container filled with bright flowering plants.

The lean-to conservatory against the house wall takes up little space and links the house to the garden. An extended range of tender plants can be grown in this as it provides additional warmth and shelter.

A small lawn provides a contrast of texture and colour. Gravel is prevented from migrating on to it by a hard edging of stone, and containers are positioned on the gravel side of the edging to soften it and to link the lawn and gravel areas. The lawn itself is shaded and made more secluded by the shrubs that are planted around it, and their lush growth is a fine contrast with the gravel.

Small containers with visually exciting plants, such as *Phormium cookianum* subsp. *hookeri* 'Cream Delight' and *Lilium davidii*, are used on the area between the raised brick patio and the house wall to provide planting that is controlled but interesting. If necessary they can be moved to the patio or into the conservatory for overwintering.

The oval bed, which is edged with rough chunks of stone, is richly planted with a variety of plants that come into flower sequentially over a long period to provide an ever-changing focal feature. This is complemented by a small semicircular bed against the wall.

Placing a single paver in the gravel adds a surprise element. It breaks up what could potentially be a rather large, uninteresting stretch of gravel, and it could be used as a platform for a container if you wish.

The water feature is very simple – a sink with gently flowing spout running into it – but it adds the gentle sound of water and creates a focal point in the part of the garden near the garage wall.

PLANTING

The planting in this garden is restricted to relatively small concentrations, rather than being in borders around the edges, but it is effective and does not rely on flowers alone for colour. Foliage interest is provided by the rich, deep reds of the plants on the patio, including *Ajuga reptans* 'Catlin's Giant', and the textures and shades of green of the lawn and shrub bed.

One or two climbers are used to clothe the top of the far wall and a trellis guides a climber up the house wall near the lawn, but for the most part the walls are left bare to accentuate the planting and to keep the eye within the garden.

The tall *Trachycarpus fortunei* (Chusan palm), with its interesting spiky foliage, is planted in the far corner to create a visually compelling feature to draw the eye. Flowers in the main shrub bed are largely white to provide contrast with the greenery.

opposite: This gravel garden is planted with sun-lovers such as iris and eucalyptus, the gritty surface punctuated by smooth white stones and spiky *Sempervivum* (houseleeks) grown in pots.

above: The spiky foliage of *Trachycarpus fortunei* provides an unusual high-level focal point for a gravel garden.

TIPS FOR GRAVEL GARDENS

• Place a porous membrane under the gravel to suppress weeds
• The gravel should be at least 3cm (1in) deep
• Make sure that the gravel is contained so that it does not migrate to areas where it could be a problem
• Lay gravel on a good base of hardcore and sand
• Keep gravel weed free and clean or it loses its effect
• Do not choose gravel that is too small and remember that it will look more stylish if it is a single colour and the same size
• For a softer effect, the raised patio could be made from wood

WOODLAND GARDEN

The emphasis in this heavily textural garden is on seclusion, privacy and tranquillity. Seating in which to relax can be placed on the grass in the 'woodland glade', or on the sunny paved patio close to the house.

PLANTING KEY

1 *Pelargonium* Tornado Series
2 *Phormium tenax* 'Variegatum'
3 *Heuchera* 'Palace Purple'
4 *Hedera hibernica* (syn. *H. helix* subsp. *hibernica*)
5 *Hydrangea anomala* subsp. *petiolaris* (syn. *H. petiolaris*)
6 *Lonicera etrusca* 'Superba'
7 *Forsythia* x *intermedia* 'Lynwood'
8 *Primula vulgaris* 'Double Sulphur'
9 *Hebe rakaiensis*
10 *Salvia officinalis* 'Icterina'
11 *Pittosporum tenuifolium* 'Irene Paterson'
12 *Fagus sylvatica* 'Purpurea Pendula'
13 *Lavatera* 'Burgundy Wine'
14 *Quercus pontica*
15 *Digitalis purpurea* Excelsior Group
16 *Hydrangea quercifolia* 'Snow Flake' (syn. *H. quercifolia* 'Flore Pleno')
17 *Corylus avellana*
18 *Magnolia* 'Iolanthe'
19 *Sorbus aucuparia*
20 *Elaeagnus* x *ebbingei* 'Gilt Edge'
21 *Garrya elliptica* 'James Roof'
22 *Robinia pseudoacacia* 'Frisia'
23 *Betula ermanii*
24 *Malus* 'Butterball'
25 *Fagus sylvatica*
26 *Prunus padus* 'Watereri'
27 *Filipendula palmata*
28 *Mahonia aquifolium*
29 *Acer griseum*
30 *Ilex* 'Brilliant'
31 *Laburnum anagyroides*
32 *Ulmus procera*
33 *Crataegus laevigata* 'Plena' (syn. *C. laevigata* 'Flore Pleno')
34 *Betula pendula*
35 *Milium effusum* 'Aureum'
36 *Luzula sylvatica* 'Marginata' (syn. *L. sylvatica* 'Aureomarginata')
37 *Daphne laureola*
38 *Syringa vulgaris*
39 *Cornus alba* 'Elegantissima'
40 *Carpinus betulus*
41 *Prunus spinosa*
42 *Laurus nobilis*
43 *Rosa rugosa*
44 *Lavandula angustifolia* 'Munstead'
45 *Helleborus argutifolius* (syn. *H. corsicus*)

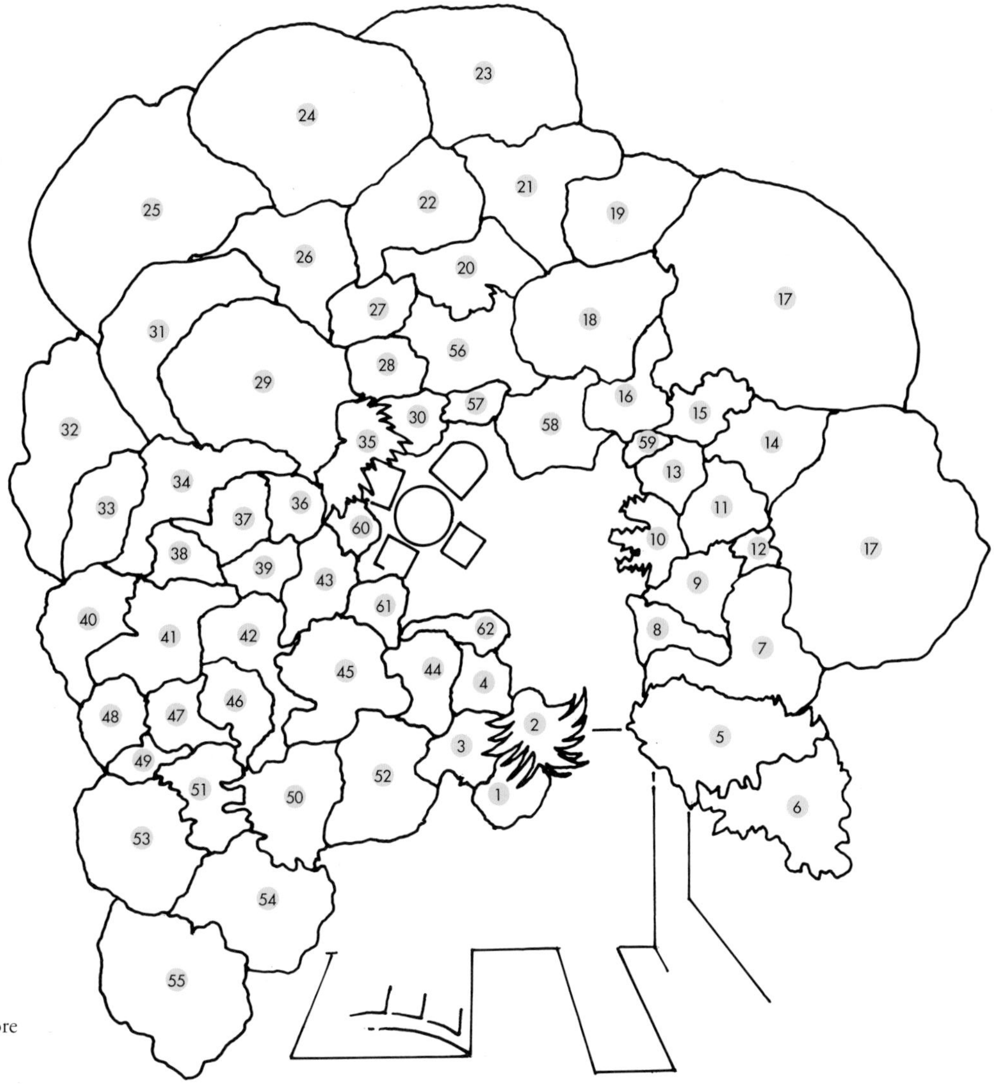

46 *Spiraea japonica* 'Little Princess'
47 *Berberis darwinii* 'Flame'
48 *Philadelphus* 'Dame Blanche'
49 *Cotoneaster* 'Cornubia'
50 *Berberis* 'Goldilocks'
51 *Rosa* 'Paul's Scarlet Climber'
52 *Rosa* 'Ferdy' (syn. *R.* 'Keitoli')
53 *Rosa* 'Climbing Iceberg'
54 *Rosa filipes* 'Kiftsgate'
55 *Rosa* 'Golden Showers'

56 *Crocus pulchellus*
57 *Narcissus* 'Beryl'
58 *Anemone nemorosa*
59 *Viola odorata*
60 *Crocus speciosus* 'Oxonian'
61 *Oxalis lobata*
62 *Centaurea cyanus*

56, 57 and 58 planted at random at the edges of the lawn

nious garden that will be a joy to come home to all year round. This garden is easy to create and will provide a spiritual rest from the busy world, changing subtly with each season but always providing colour and texture.

FEATURES

The only formal feature in this garden is the paved patio, which is adjacent to the house. It is constructed from large, plain paving stones and provides a warm and sunny seating area. It also serves as a break between the shrubs, which are the main feature of the planting, and the house. Two shallow steps from the patio allow descent to the lawn, which is on a slightly lower level. The proportion of hard paving to lawn is about one-third paving to two-thirds lawn, which is appropriate for a site of this size.

The lawn is shaded, but not so much that it stays cool and damp, and it is an ideal area for alfresco eating. The furniture is lightweight and can be easily moved from the lawn to the patio for a change of scene. It is white to provide contrast and interest. The grass seed is a mixture that is selected to withstand some wear and tear and also to do well in shade, and the lawn is kept lightly mown and not too short.

PLANTING

The plants around the grassy space lend this garden its woodland feel. The boundaries are totally disguised by the plants, and their branches overhang the lawn, creating areas of dappled shade and masking the edge of the lawn. Movable pots are used to introduce plants to the patio area, and a planted urn marks the change in level of the steps and also reduces the width of the approach into the lawn area, emphasizing the sense of entering a woodland clearing.

The range of shrubs and other woodland plants means that there is constant changing interest throughout the year. Woodland plants tend to be tall and strong growing or small and shade loving, and it is important to

THE FOCAL POINT OF THIS GARDEN is the lawn, which is surrounded by taller planting in deep shrub borders, making it resemble a woodland clearing. The height of the planting also provides privacy and gives the garden a secluded air.

The basic layout of the garden is geometrical, but the patterns are softened and elongated to blend together. The strength of the design lies in the way the different elements of lawn, shrubs, trees, flowers and spacious patio have been combined to create a harmo-

choose plants that flower at different times to provide interest throughout the year.

A mix of deciduous and evergreen shrubs provides an ever-changing pattern of colours that is both natural and easy on the eyes, while the lush growth and darker shadows of the beds create a sense of intrigue and mystery. Native species have been chosen, because they will thrive in these conditions and create a natural-looking garden. Lower growing woodland plants are used in the area nearer the house to introduce variety and colour and to prevent the house from looking swamped. Plants that have berries and fruit will attract birds and other small visitors to complete the woodland atmosphere.

A walk in the garden brings many surprises, with herbs and shade-loving woodland plants among the more usual ones. The front of the far border has been planted with shade-loving plants, such as *Luzula sylvatica* 'Marginata' (greater woodrush), to make the most of this sheltered spot. Wildflowers have been sown in areas of rough grass at the sides to lessen the need to mow and fill the gaps left by overhanging plants.

The paved area makes it possible to include container-grown plants that would not suit the shadier parts. The containers,

which can be moved to exactly where they are needed, are filled with plants such as bright pelargoniums, but they could equally be filled with grasses in order to extend the woodland theme or with bright annuals to give splashes of colour. The mass of shrubs and climbing roses near the windows is set off by the large shrubs behind them and helps the planting to make the transition from dense lush greenery to the lighter feel of the patio area, while the climbing plants on the wall by the window bring the garden right up to the house.

Placing a brightly coloured small tree, such as *Robinia pseudoacacia* 'Frisia', at the far end of the garden will draw the eye towards the far boundary, emphasizing the length of the garden. Winter-flowering shrubs, such as *Daphne laureola*, are used to provide colour before the spring bulbs come into flower, and white-flowering plants, including *Hydrangea quercifolia* 'Snow Flake', are used as highlights against the dark green background and to create additional points of interest.

opposite: The 'woodland clearing' in this garden provides the perfect spot for a table, chairs and white-painted cast iron bench set into the lush green planting.

above right: A thickly planted, curving border flows naturally into a shady 'woodland' area of taller planting.

TIPS FOR WOODLAND GARDENS

- Plant bulbs, such as crocus, *Anemone nemorosa* (wood anemone), narcissus (daffodil) and *Eranthis hyemalis* (winter aconite), for spring interest and colour
- Use plants that will thrive in wooded, shady sites, many of which are hard to grow in sunny borders
- Prune trees and shrubs to keep the canopy light and avoid pockets of still air where fungal spores can thrive
- Trim back branches that overhang too much or that are too low to avoid bare patches developing in the lawn
- Larger, mature new shrubs will do better than small purchases because they will be able to compete and get established
- Mulch around new plants and between shrubs to keep weeds at bay
- Add wooden animals and characters to create a fairy-tale feel or to complement the woodland

SHRUB GARDEN

Curving brickwork and changes of level, contrasting foliage and dazzling flowers combine to create an imaginative and striking garden in this square space. Individual raised beds offer the opportunity to grow favourite plants with a range of soil requirements.

PLANTING KEY

1 *Salvia officinalis* 'Tricolor'
2 *Hydrangea* 'Preziosa' (syn. *H. serrata* 'Preziosa')
3 *Lonicera nitida* 'Baggesen's Gold'
4 *Sarcococca ruscifolia*
5 *Hebe* 'Bowles's Hybrid' (syn. *H.* 'Bowles's Variety')
6 *Brachyglottis greyi* (syn. *Senecio greyi*)
7 *Cornus alba* 'Siberica' (syn. *C. alba* 'Westonbirt')
8 *Forsythia suspensa*
9 *Skimmia japonica*
10 *Ribes sanguineum* 'Brocklebankii'
11 *Pieris floribunda*
12 *Stachys byzantina* (syn. *S. lanata*)
13 *Euonymus fortunei* 'Emerald 'n' Gold'
14 *Nepeta x faassenii* (syn. *N. mussinii*)
15 *Hebe* 'Blue Clouds'
16 *Salvia* 'Purple Majesty'
17 *Hebe* 'Autumn Glory'
18 *Hydrangea macrophylla* 'Lilacina'
19 *Buddleja globosa*
20 *Berberis x frikartii*
21 *Hebe albicans*
22 *Ceanothus* 'Burkwoodii'
23 *Senecio cineraria* 'Silver Dusk'
24 *Daphne jasminea*
25 *Amherstia nobilis*
26 *Rhododendron argyrophyllum*
27 *Azalea* 'Palestrina'
28 *Rosa rugosa*
29 *Azalea* 'Beethoven'
30 *Gaultheria procumbens*
31 *Gaultheria mucronata* (syn. *Pernettya mucronata*)
32 *Campanula carpatica* 'Bressingham White'
33 *Azalea* 'Kirin'
34 *Rhododendron* 'Golden Torch'
35 *Skimmia japonica* 'Rubella'
36 *Rhododendron* 'Revlon'
37 *Calluna vulgaris* 'Dark Beauty'
38 *Kalmia latifolia*
39 *Trillium grandiflorum*
40 *Rosmarinus officinalis*
41 *Ginkgo biloba*
42 *Cornus alba* 'Elegantissima'
43 *Tamarix tetrandra*
44 *Gleditsia triacanthos* 'Sunburst'
45 *Juniperus communis* 'Compressa'
46 *Salvia elegans*
47 *Camellia japonica* 'Tricolor' (syn. *C.* 'Tricolor Sieboldii')
48 *Choisya ternata*
49 *Camellia* 'Cornish Show'
50 *Tagetes* Solar Series
51 *Papaver orientale* 'Allegro'
52 *Santolina chamaecyparissus* (syn. *S. incana*)
53 *Azalea* 'Ballerina'
54 *Artemisia ludoviciana*
55 *Ruscus aculeatus*
56 *Ribes sanguineum* 'King Edward VII'
57 *Viburnum tinus*
58 *Lonicera fragrantissima*

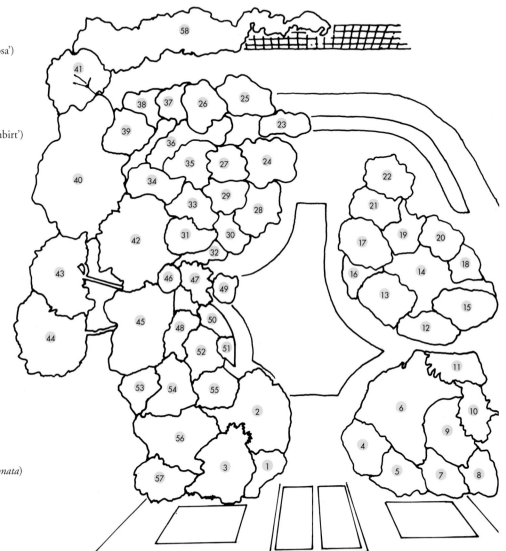

SHRUB GARDEN

THIS BROADLY SQUARE GARDEN is given dramatic appeal by having several raised beds of different heights and sizes. These not only bring variety to the garden but leave an asymmetrical, curvy lawn, which draws attention away from the symmetry and squareness of the plot.

The eye is encouraged to rove to all parts of this garden, where there is always something interesting to see. Even the imposing back wall is cleverly broken up by the slightly lower wall in front of it to bring the eye back to the garden. What could be a dark, sunken space with little light is turned into a sheltered haven with colourful plants and year-round appeal. Using a wide range of shrubs as the dominant planting not only provides interest but also makes the garden low maintenance. Once established, this garden will require very little work to keep it looking good, apart from the lawn, which will need routine care and mowing.

FEATURES

The grey bricks used to construct the walls contrast well with the foliage and show off the flowers to great effect. Because this garden faces away from the sun, the higher bank has been left free of plants to admit the greatest possible amount of light.

The small patio area is plain, and the plants come right up to the house, bringing the garden close to the living area and enticing people outdoors. The steps from the patio lead straight to the lawn, which provides the perfect cover for the central area, with the smooth green forming a strong contrast to the grey bricks and the surrounding plants. The white mowing edge and steps frame and emphasize the lawn's unusual shape, and at the same time the white line serves to unite the patio area with the rest of the garden.

Using higher raised beds at the back and lower ones at the front makes it possible to create a verdant, lush backdrop of plants and the illusion of a deep, dark boundary. The widely spaced slats in the fence provide privacy without blocking light.

PLANTING

Using shrubs with attractive foliage and planting a combination of deciduous and evergreen shrubs and small trees ensure that there are ever-changing colours and foliage interest all year. An advantage of using raised beds is that it is possible to create the right conditions for particular favourites – soil that will suit a group of acid-loving plants can be provided in an otherwise neutral garden, for example. In this scheme camellias, rhododendrons, azaleas and heathers in the corner facing the house create a blaze of colour.

The plants have been chosen for their interesting shapes, textures and colours. Low perennials are planted among the shrubs to add extra colour and interest in summer. A mix of different greens and varying leaf sizes helps to create a restful atmosphere, while the colourful corner opposite the house offers interest and, facing the sun, makes a sunny, attractive corner.

Colour in the border does not depend solely on flowers. Plants with silver or blue-tinged foliage, such as *Stachys byzantina* (lamb's ears), *Artemisia ludoviciana* (western mugwort) and *Santolina chamaecyparissus* (cotton lavender), will lighten borders and provide a variety of forms and textures, as their subtle hues and textures form a silver-blue bed.

The hard edges of the garden are obscured by selecting plants that grow towards and over them. Height is provided by plants such as *Buddleja globosa*, while summer bedding plants increase variety at ground level, and additional spring interest could be provided if wished by underplanting some of the shrubs with bulbs. One small bed has been left for annuals, to give some scope for 'pottering' and a continual change of colours in this area.

opposite: Acid-loving plants, including rhododendrons and azaleas in blazing colours, are planted in raised beds filled with the correct soil to fulfil their needs.

above left: The double-flowered form of flame-red *Rhododendron simsii* would be a good choice to add striking colour to a bed of acid-loving varieties.

above: Spiky *Stachys byzantina* and a feathery artemisia contrast with the rounded dome of a white-flowered hebe in this silvery composition.

TIPS FOR SHRUB GARDENS

- Keep the lawn mown fairly short and even to provide a level and smooth surface
- Prepare the soil well and buy good quality plants so they establish quickly
- If you can, add an irrigation system because watering will be necessary in dry periods and you will otherwise have to clamber in the beds
- Include plants with scent to create a relaxed atmosphere
- Prune and dead-head when necessary to give a long flowering season and to keep the plants in shape
- Grow acid-loving plants in containers, which can be sunk in a raised bed so that plants are grown in the correct soil and can be restricted in size

URBAN GARDEN

Clean lines and bold spaces, colour contrasts and mirror images: these are just some of the devices used to create this stunningly successful modern urban garden. The carefully considered planting enhances the overall ambience of relaxed orderliness.

PLANTING KEY

1 *Betula pendula*
2 *Hedera helix* 'Duckfoot'
3 *Juniperus squamata* 'Blue Star'
4 *Glechoma hederacea* 'Variegata'
5 *Artemisia ludoviciana*
6 *Hosta* 'Wide Brim'
7 *Galium odoratum*
8 *Thymus serpyllum* var. *coccineus*
9 *Bergenia* 'Wintermärchen'
10 *Euonymus fortunei* 'Emerald 'n' Gold'
11 *Viburnum tinus*
12 *Pittosporum tenuifolium* 'Irene Paterson'
13 *Clematis* 'Jackmanii'
14 *Philadelphus* 'Dame Blanche'
15 *Hedera helix* 'Buttercup'
16 *Hydrangea quercifolia*
17 *Festuca glauca* 'Elijah Blue'
18 *Helictotrichon sempervirens*
19 *Phormium* 'Sundowner'
20 *Yucca gloriosa* 'Variegata'
21 *Ligustrum ovalifolium*
22 *Lonicera periclymenum* 'Belgica'
23 *Cortaderia selloana* 'Pumila'
24 *Potentilla fruticosa* 'Manchu'
25 *Tellima grandiflora*
26 *Hosta fortunei* var. *albopicta*
27 *Morus nigra*
28 *Helleborus argutifolius*
29 *Hemerocallis* 'Pink Damask'
30 *Viburnum carlesii*
31 *Veronica spicata*
32 *Digitalis purpurea* Excelsior Group
33 *Pieris formosa*
34 *Laurus nobilis*
35 *Garrya elliptica* 'James Roof'
36 *Helleborus orientalis*
37 *Hebe rakaiensis*
38 *Robinia pseudoacacia* 'Frisia'
39 *Lavatera* 'Barnsley'
40 *Pyracantha atalantioides* 'Aurea' (syn. *P. gibbsii* 'Flava')
41 *Sedum spectabile* 'Brilliant'
42 *Phyllostachys nigra*
43 *Lonicera japonica*
44 *Fuchsia* 'Tom Thumb'
45 *Verbascum* 'Helen Johnson'
46 *Clematis macropetala* 'Markham's Pink'
47 *Wisteria sinensis*
48 *Hakonechloa macra* 'Aureola'

49 *Agave americana* 'Variegata'
50 *Imperata cylindrica* 'Rubra' (syn. *I. cylindrica* 'Red Baron')
51 *Ruta graveolens*
52 *Clematis montana* var. *rubens* 'Elizabeth'

53 *Skimmia japonica* 'Nymans'
54 *Lagurus ovatus*
55 *Syringa meyeri* var. *spontanea* 'Palibin'
56 *Jasminum officinale* 'Aureum'

Strong lines, symmetry and balance are used to create this stunning garden. The length is broken up in an innovative way by using two interlocking circles of lawn.

The strong design reflects an individual character. There is a good balance of greenery and space as well as reflections of the features contained within it, and what could be an ordinary urban garden is transformed into an intriguing, interesting area that is an invitation to explore and at the same time a scheme that provides a feeling of peace and harmony.

FEATURES

The hard landscaping uses three main types of material: small pavers, bricks and gravel. The gravel is divided into two bands of colour on each side, divided by a line of white bricks, which are continued to form the edges of the circular lawns. The lush green of the lawns contrasts with the gravel around them, and they are set in relief by the border of white bricks running continuously around them. The bricks form a path that could also be used as a track for cycles if there are children in the garden.

The pale blue of the gravel areas beside the patio contrasts beautifully with the deep grey of the pavers on the patio itself. Using the same materials but in different colours is a good way of introducing change to a garden and can be striking, especially if broken up with bricks, as here, in a colour that contrasts with both colours used. The white bricks provide strong lines of definition, and complement the blue, cream and green of the gravel and lawn.

Apart from the plants there is very little ornamentation in this garden. The combination of clean lines and space is maintained throughout the garden until you reach the rear boundary, which is deep, dark and lush and provides privacy. The white wall at the far end will be glimpsed through the shrubs, giving the illusion of space beyond the garden. Because it is white it will reflect sunlight and subtly foreshorten the garden to the eye, further reducing the appearance of length.

The fence is topped by straight-edged trellis and clothed in mainly evergreen climbers for added privacy.

TIPS FOR URBAN GARDENS

- Use a good quality lawn mix to maintain a lush, green sward to contrast with the edging and gravel
- Cut back hedges regularly and frequently to keep them thick and bushy
- Sweep and turn the gravel yearly to keep it looking fresh and clean and replace areas that get dirty or mossy
- Keep the patio uncluttered and use non-slip stones
- Use a different combination of colours for the edge, gravel areas and patio to create a different ambience

definition and order to produce an overall air of relaxed order.

The pergola is framed by well-clipped privet hedges, and it cannot be seen fully until you are halfway down the garden, yet the stepping stones can be seen to indicate there is something there, adding surprise and intrigue. This is the only feature, apart from the statue, that is not mirrored.

The furniture is steel, which is in keeping with the modern style of this garden and reflects both the grey of the pavers and the material used for the statue.

The essence of this garden is bold simplicity. There are only four containers, but they are striking blue lead and hold evergreen trailing and ornamental plants.

FEATURES

The gravelled area is largely unplanted except for bold grasses in clusters and one or two architecturally interesting plants, such as Phormium 'Sundowner' and Yucca gloriosa 'Variegata'. Placing the grass clumps in alternate rows to the shrubs gives a pattern that enforces the well-organized and bold feel of this garden.

Well-spaced shrubs along the bases of the side walls accentuate the ordered feel to the garden while their unclipped forms counter the formality.

Every feature in the garden, apart from the focal point of the statue, has a mirror image of its shape placed somewhere in the garden. The small fountain, for example, is mirrored in shape by a graceful *Betula pendula* (silver birch), grown on the opposite side of the patio. The trees in the far corners reflect each other in both form and shape, but because the species are different, nothing is repeated precisely.

The lawns curve away towards the rear of the garden into a deep bed of shrubs and low-growing, shade-loving plants. Using circular lawns adds a sense of width to the garden by drawing the eye across it and towards the edges, thereby breaking up the long view to the far end. The eye is also drawn to a steel statue at the far end of the lawns. This is an individual touch, which entices you into the garden, and it also cleverly leaves a curvy outline for the outer beds, and this further breaks up the long shape. There is a great deal of balance and symmetry in this garden, while the strong curves provide sharp

opposite: This lawn is edged with bricks and surrounded by gravel for a contrast of colours and textures. The curved seat echoes the line of the lawn.

above left: A bold *Agave americana* 'Variegata' is perfect for a modern urban garden.

above: A small bubble fountain in a simple bowl sits well among a collection of plants with contrasting foliage.

SEMI-FORMAL SQUARE GARDEN

Massed planting in raised beds and containers, and against walls and trellis, contrasts with symmetrical elements and squared paving to produce a semi-formal design for this small garden. Slatted wooden furniture, incorporating right angles and straight lines, enhances the overall feel of relaxed formality.

PLANTING KEY

1 *Vitis davidii*
2 *Ceanothus* 'Burkwoodii'
3 *Viburnum plicatum* 'Pink Beauty'
4 *Sorbaria tomentosa* var. *angustifolia*
5 *Veronica spicata* 'Barcarolle'
6 *Narcissus* 'Portrush'
7 *Phormium* 'Dazzler'
8 *Agave americana* 'Marginata'
9 *Lonicera fragrantissima*
10 *Jasminum officinale*
11 *Hebe cupressoides*
12 *Mentha spicata* (syn. *M. viridis*)
13 *Vinca major* 'Reticulata'
14 *Phoenix roebelenii*
15 *Festuca glauca* 'Elijah Blue'
16 *Linum flavum* 'Compactum'
17 *Narcissus* 'Suzy'
18 *Melissa officinalis*
19 *Verbascum olympicum*
20 *Phlomis fruticosa*
21 *Paeonia wittmanniana*
22 *Narcissus* 'Ice Follies'
23 *Magnolia sargentiana*
24 *Liquidambar orientalis*
25 *Tulipa urumiensis*
26 *Narcissus* 'Yellow Cheerfulness'
27 *Hemerocallis* 'Scarlock'
28 *Rosmarinus officinalis* 'Benenden Blue'
29 *Bougainvillea* 'Dania'
30 *Tulipa* 'Oxford'
31 *Begonia* 'Pin-up'
32 *Petunia* Polo Series
33 *Sempervivum montanum*
34 *Eremurus stenophyllus*
35 *Veronica gentianoides*
36 *Agapanthus campanulatus*
37 *Hebe* 'Simon Delaux'
38 *Hedera helix* 'Adam'
39 *Hechtia glomerata*
40 *Heliotropium* 'Marine'
41 *Geranium erianthum*
42 *Lobelia erinus* Cascade Series
43 *Lobelia erinus* 'Lilac Fountain'
44 *Verbascum chaixii* 'Gainsborough'
45 *Hosta* 'Antioch'
46 *Acer griseum*
47 *Aristolochia littoralis* (syn. *A. elegans*)
48 *Fabiana imbricata* 'Prostata'
49 *Papaver orientale* 'Mrs Perry'
50 *Myrteola nummularia*
51 *Drimys lanceolata*
52 *Angelica archangelica*
53 *Buglossoides purpurocaerulea* (syn. *Lithospermum purpureocaeruleum*
54 *Euonymus fortunei* 'Minimus'
55 *Euonymus fortunei* 'Emerald 'n' Gold'

SEMI-FORMAL SQUARE GARDEN

THE SEMI-FORMAL NATURE of this garden comes from the fact that it is designed around a geometrical shape and all the paving and raised beds are symmetrical. The garden is balanced by the chairs, set diagonally to emphasize the axis, and by the planters either side of the seat. The other corners are softened by containers and planting so it is formal, yet not formal.

Every available surface is used for growing plants, and there is even trellis along the tops of the walls so that plants can soften every area. Using raised beds of different depths and sizes introduces dramatic changes of level and allows for a huge variety of planting within the small area. The deep beds at the rear of the garden and along the sides allow larger shrubs and plants to create a sense of privacy.

There is no one dominant feature in this garden. Rather, the eye is led to all areas, and visitors to the garden are drawn to each area for subtly different reasons.

FEATURES

The uniform, cream-coloured paving stones create a central area that is light and airy, and their square shape subtly reinforces the shape of the site. They reflect light and create an open, welcoming feel.

The frosted glass window on the right-hand side of the garden provides shelter without shade on the patio and screens an unattractive view. It emphasizes the boundary while allowing in lots of light. Two windowboxes attached to the wall bring flowers up to the level of the bottom of the window. Because the garden is small a permanent structure is not practical, but shade is adequately provided by a small tree. Even the top of the wall has containers along it to raise the level of screening and add variety. These

PLANTING

Plants cover every wall to link the garden to the house and beckon you into the space to explore. The group of larger containers by the door hides an area of the garden from view, creating intrigue and encouraging a desire to investigate further.

The two trees, *Betula pendula* (silver birch) and *Acer griseum* (paper-bark maple), although of different genera, have the same habit and periods of interest and balance each other. At all sides, plants spill out from the raised beds and planting areas into the garden, and containers are randomly placed to offset the formality and create a pretty, semi-formal garden with an ordered but relaxed feel to it.

The shape and form of the plants is varied, and there are lots of colours to create an ever-changing canvas and bring each area of the garden into its own over the year. Some unusual and stunning plants, including *Phoenix roebelenii* (pygmy date palm), lend themselves to this semi-formal setting. Plants with spiky shapes, like *Phormium* 'Dazzler' and *Agave americana* 'Marginata', contrast with the tumbling, softer nature of their neighbours. The grass *Festuca glauca* 'Elijah Blue' in a pot adds a touch of elegance to the shady area.

The flower colours are largely pale shades to help to create a spacious feel, but there are also splashes of bright colour to create contrast, and one or two focal plants are in containers to provide talking points and appealing contrasts. Several scented climbers will allow their scent to drift on the air in the enclosed space on summer days.

A grapevine, *Vitis davidii*, grown on trellis attached to the house wall will smother the brickwork with foliage and produce small bunches of delicious grapes later in the year. Planting against the glass screen is kept light, to allow maximum light through and create dappled shade in the garden.

Containers hold a range of plants, from masses of bright annuals to single formal plants. These can be grouped or dotted around to create different moods or just for a change. The mix of formal plants, such as the majestic vertical spires of *Eremurus stenophyllus* and *Verbascum chaixii* 'Gainsborough', planted near trailing evergreens, flowers and shrubs creates a disordered yet harmonious feel to the beds and contrasts beautifully with the formality of the paving slabs.

are filled with exciting and colourful plants to encourage the eye upwards.

The furniture, which is all white-painted wood to create a sense of unity, is positioned so that the welcoming table and bench are opposite the doorway, enticing visitors into the garden and creating the feel of another room added to the house.

opposite: Simple wooden furniture and square paving slabs are surrounded by rich planting and colourful containers in this semi-formal garden.

above left: Annual *Lathyrus odoratus* climbing up above tender pelargoniums can be used to provide temporary height and colour in containers until the permanent plantings mature.

TIPS FOR SEMI-FORMAL GARDENS

- Choose unusual plants for interest
- A group of containers can be as effective as a flowerbed and can be moved around if you want a change
- Wooden furniture looks more inviting than plastic
- For temporary colours and scents until the main plants are established grow annuals, such as *Lathyrus odoratus* (sweet pea) in containers
- Use materials such as small, brightly coloured bricks to make the raised walls to contrast with the pavers

INFORMAL RECTANGULAR GARDEN

An informal picture is created by disguising the shape of this rectangular garden with soft planting in borders, raised beds and containers. The furniture on the patio mirrors the design of an ornate white bench that provides a focal point at the end of the lawn.

PLANTING KEY

1   *Wisteria sinensis*
2   *Campanula medium* 'Bells of Holland'
3   *Begonia* 'Olympia White'
4   *Thymus pulegioides* 'Aureus' (syn. *T. x citriodorus* 'Aureus')
5   *Laurus nobilis*
6   *Phormium tenax* 'Variegatum'
7   *Brassica oleracea* Osaka Series
8   *Fascicularia bicolor* (syn. *F. pitcairniifolia*)
9   *Eryngium variifolium*
10 *Lavatera thuringiaca*
11 *Delphinium* 'Rosemary Brock'
12 *Erythronium* 'Pagoda'
13 *Phormium* 'Sundowner'
14 *Discocactus horstii*
15 *Woodsia polystichoides*
16 *Pittosporum tenuifolium* 'Deborah'
17 *Phlox paniculata* 'Balmoral'
18 *Desmodium yunnanense* (syn. *D. praestans*)
19 *Photinia* x *fraseri* 'Birmingham'
20 *Deutzia gracilis*
21 *Magnolia* x *soulangeana* 'Lennei'
22 *Rosa* 'Crimson Shower'
23 *Pieris floribunda*
24 *Rosa* 'Conservation' (syn. *R.* 'Cocdimple')
25 *Rosmarinus officinalis*
26 *Hydrangea macrophylla* 'Altona'
27 *Philadelphus* 'Belle Etoile'
28 *Sedum spectabile* 'Brilliant'
29 *Senecio viravira* (syn. *S. leucostachys*)
30 *Saponaria* 'Bressingham'
31 *Ligularia przewalskii* (syn. *Senecio przewalskii*)
32 *Hemerocallis* 'Tonia Gay'
33 *Daphne odora*
34 *Ficus deltoidea*
35 *Phillyrea latifolia*
36 *Clematis* 'Nelly Moser'
37 *Crocus* and *Narcissus* spring bulbs underplanted at front of beds

THE STRONG RECTANGULAR SHAPE of the garden is reinforced by the choice of paving stones, bricks, steps and patterns, but the shape of the plot is then deliberately obscured by having lots of plants overflowing on to the lawn to hide the straight lines. Harsh angles are cleverly softened with shrubs and raised beds, and curves and some pretty features are introduced to draw attention away from the overall shape. The tumbling, trailing nature of many of the shrubs lends the garden an air of playful informality, but the underlying shape of the plot is maintained, while all the harsh edges and corners are disguised by clever design and carefully chosen plants to create a stunningly pretty and enjoyable garden.

FEATURES

The awning on the patio provides shade on warm days and is a colourful feature in its own right. The garden furniture is white-coated cast iron, as is the seat on the lawn, which is the main focal feature of this garden. Placed at the far end of the garden, the pretty, ornate seat draws the eye down the plot and away from the neighbouring buildings. The seat, in turn, is situated so as to receive the sun, and from it the best view of the garden can be obtained. The borders along the sides are deep to create a sense of seclusion and give privacy.

The steps that lead from the patio down to the lawn are bordered by curved, raised beds. These beds narrow the entrance to the lawn, which then opens out, giving a real sense of a separate area within the garden. The division created by the raised beds softens the plain, angular line of the garden and also allows the planting to continue right up to the house. The semicircular raised bed under the window serves to complete the link between garden and house and raises the plants to eye level for people on the patio. The random use of containers on the patio gives a sense of informality, and the containers on the steps also serve to link the two main areas together.

The steps are in the same stone as the mowing edge of the lawn. The hard landscaping materials are in shades of white and grey, which add an airy feel to the garden. The furniture and railing next to the steps are white, to complement the grey chosen for the paving and add lightness to the overall scheme of the garden.

The small shed will soon be covered in foliage and colour as the scrambling rose covers it in leaves and flowers. It would also be possible to place a trellis screen in front of it to provide a more permanent disguise.

PLANTING

The plants that have been selected for the borders and raised beds are soft and pretty, and they have long flowering periods to extend the seasons of interest. Including small shrubs and plants that bear brightly coloured flowers among the larger deciduous and evergreen shrubs will bring continual subtle changes in the garden throughout the year against the permanent backcloth of rich green. Mixed planting always adds lots of year-round interest, and every plant in this small space justifies its selection by displaying an interesting characteristic or having a long flowering season.

The shape of many of the plants is rounded – even the flowers of *Hydrangea macrophylla* 'Altona' are borne in round, soft corymbs – and their habits are anything but formal.

The well-maintained lawn is a perfect contrast to the bright, colourful, rolling shapes of the planting in the borders, which, in their turn, make a relaxed contrast with the straight lines of the plot and effectively remove the potential for it to be rather austere in appearance.

A few plants in colourful containers are all that is needed on the patio, and these can be filled with annuals or specimen plants and moved around. Indoor plants, such as cacti, can be stood outside during the summer provided they are positioned where their spines will not cause problems. The canopy projecting from the house, with the climber above it, creates a café-like atmosphere and provides an ideal shady place to eat out. Dainty plants that might get lost in the main beds are grown in the semicircular raised bed, where they will receive plenty of attention. Alternatively, this is an ideal place for herbs, which will provide scent on the patio as well as ingredients for the kitchen.

Elsewhere the plants are easy to look after, and the fronts of the beds are planted with perennials and spring bulbs to provide splashes of colour from early spring right through to late autumn.

Disguising the boundaries with plants removes clues to the garden's size and shape

and so it appears to have no clear limits. This frees the mind to indulge in the illusion of endless space. It is an illusion, but a very effective one, and the impression of space is furthered by the large variety of climbing plants that disguise the walls and clothe them with foliage and colour. The climbers create a green background, which is both natural and gives seclusion.

Although the planting around the lawn is limited to the comparatively narrow beds, which seem to emphasize the linear shape, the two large rounded beds part-way along the garden and the soft planting effectively counter any formal feel.

opposite: The clean lines of the rectangular lawns and flight of steps emphasize the shape and length of this informally planted garden.

above left: Climbers like this *Clematis* 'Dawn' entwined with honeysuckle can be used lavishly to blur the boundaries of an informal garden.

above: A decorative white-coated cast iron seat creates a focal point that can be positioned to draw the eye in a required direction – perhaps to guide it away from an eyesore, or to emphasize a particular vista.

TIPS FOR INFORMAL GARDENS

- Strong geometric hard landscaping can be softened by billowing, informal planting
- In a small plot make sure every plant or feature earns its place by having a long season of interest
- Use light-coloured materials to give a sense of lightness and space
- Choose plants with colourful flowers to hold the attention in the garden and prevent the eye wandering to less attractive features beyond
- Keep down weeds by using a mulch, so that plants get established easily with less competition and quickly create the desired garden

L-SHAPED GARDEN

The difficult shape of this garden has been turned to advantage by a clever design, which both softens the line of the 'L' and links the two areas together, drawing the visitor on to explore further. The planting is at once elegant and exciting, complementing the simple materials used for the hard landscaping.

PLANTING KEY

1 *Hedera helix* 'Buttercup'
2 *Hibiscus syriacus* 'Oiseau Bleu' (syn. *H. syriacus* 'Bluebird')
3 *Verbena rigida* 'Polaris'
4 *Hydrangea quercifolia* 'Snow Flake' (syn. *H. quercifolia* 'Flore Pleno')
5 *Hosta fortunei* var. *albopicta* (syn. *H.* 'Aureomaculata')
6 *Eucalyptus delegatensis*
7 *Cornus alba* 'Elegantissima'
8 *Salvia officinalis* 'Kew Gold'
9 *Mahonia aquifolium* 'Orange Flame'
10 *Escallonia* 'Langleyensis'
11 *Lupinus arboreus* 'Snow Queen'
12 *Fraxinus ornus*
13 *Deutzia x hybrida* 'Mont Rose'
14 *Daphne mezereum*
15 *Mentha suaveolens* (syn. *M. rotundifolia*)
16 *Philadelphus* 'Belle Etoile'
17 *Davidia involucrata*
18 *Mentha requienii* (syn. *M. corsica*)
19 *Molinia caerulea* subsp. *arundinacea* 'Karl Foerster'
20 *Tulipa* 'Dreaming Maid'
21 *Malus* 'Candied Apple' (syn. *M.* 'Weeping Candied Apple')
22 *Fritillaria meleagris*
23 *Prunus* 'Hally Jolivette'
24 *Dryopteris filix-mas* 'Barnesii'
25 *Cotoneaster lacteus*
26 *Scrophularia auriculata* 'Variegata' (syn. *S. nodosa* var. *variegata*)
27 *Hebe* 'Autumn Glory'
28 *Santolina pinnata* (syn. *S. chamaecyparissus* subsp. *tomentosa*)
29 *Hemerocallis* 'Apple Tart'
30 *Heliotropium* 'Marine'
31 *Veronica longifolia* 'Blauriesin' (syn. *V. longifolia* 'Blue Giantess')
32 *Fargesia murieliae* (syn. *Sinarundinaria murieliae*)
33 *Phormium* 'Maori Sunrise' (syn. *P. tenax* 'Rainbow Sunrise')
34 *Narcissus* mixed
35 *Crocus* mixed

34 and **35** underplanted in beds for spring colour near the house

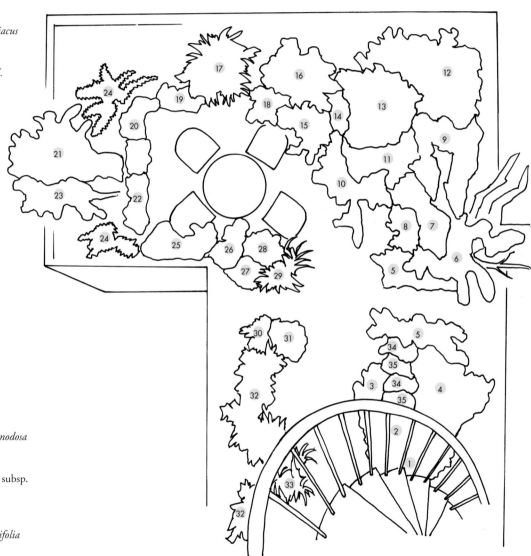

ALTHOUGH THIS GARDEN is a strong L shape, the space in the central area has been formed into a curve, thereby softening the impact of the rather angular plot. The bold, linear design integrates the two parts of the garden, and the use of the same paving material for both parts further links and unites the two areas.

The design uses the change of level as a natural divide. The lower area is planted with easy-care shrubs and plants to give lots of foliage interest and colour, while the upper part is a secluded, pretty sitting area. The pattern of bright white squares edged with tiny red bricks is striking, creating a well-defined surface that makes a strong design statement carried through both parts of the garden. Keeping the hard landscaping in geometrical lines and softening it with lush and varied plants provides the ideal solution to this potentially puzzling shape, and makes this garden inviting and interesting.

FEATURES

Although the garden is based largely on squares and rectangles, the hard edges are softened by the use of plants that will grow over and around them.

The materials chosen contrast strongly with each other and, because the flooring is so dazzling, the number of different surfaces is limited. The high walls, which act as a windbreak and offer privacy, are painted white, to show off the foliage and reflect light into the garden. The steps between the two levels are grey to complement those descending to ground level from the flat above.

Light is used well in this garden, with the open central area strongly reflecting sunlight. This contrasts with the cool, shady corner created by *Escallonia* 'Langleyensis', *Fraxinus ornus* and *Deutzia* x *hybrida* 'Mont Rose' and the deep green of the shrubs. An overlooked corner has been densely planted with taller shrubs to create privacy and shade. White pavers reflect the light and make the garden seem spacious and airy.

Eucalyptus delegatensis, the tall, angular *Hemerocallis* 'Sugar Cookie' and the easy poise of *Fargesia murieliae* (umbrella bamboo) to the gentle elegance of the ferns, there is a wonderful mixture of shapes, texture and colour, providing constant interest everywhere you look. Who needs lots of colours and textures in the materials when you have this much excitement in the planting?

The raised beds by the steps serve to lift the planting easily to the higher level, helping the eye to travel from one area to the other. The unplanted urn, placed on the wall, provides an attractive focal point halfway along the garden.

In the higher part of the garden, some aromatic plants are used to create a fragrant atmosphere and a relaxed feel. Spring and summer bulbs are used to provide masses of colour in different areas over a prolonged period so that the garden will always be interesting and inviting.

The small trees, ferns and raised side beds used in this part of the garden are in direct contrast to the rangier, less organized planting in the rest of the garden, and using different types of planting in each 'leg' of the plot clearly differentiates between the two areas, which are nevertheless firmly linked by the paving.

It is important to have strong design elements at the point where the two parts of

the garden meet. In this case, the deep, rich planting of larger shrubs gives a reason to walk to the end of the garden to see the rest of it, and the *Davidia involucrata* (pocket handkerchief tree) will really draw the eye to this point of the garden with its amazing flowers in spring. The uneven white bracts, which look like hundreds of tiny handkerchiefs, will form a beautiful contrast with the light green foliage and will always provide a talking point.

PLANTING

By heavily disguising the boundaries with planting, the awkward shape of the plot is effectively lost, yet the garden retains the surprise of having a hidden area. Planting is confined largely to the edges, but interest is created by introducing variation into the depths of the beds, and bamboos are included because their elegant, tall, narrow shapes break up the walls.

L-shaped gardens provide the ideal opportunity to create surprises, and the beautiful small trees and ferns in the raised bed behind the seating area will be a delightful find. From the house, the chairs and table can just be glimpsed, giving the illusion of space and confirming the existence of another part to the garden.

Although the hard landscaping uses only a few different materials and textures, the same cannot be said for the plants in this garden. From the blue-grey oval leaves of

opposite: Descending these spiral steps into the garden below allows the visitor to catch glimpses of its delights before reaching ground level.

above: A bold pattern of light-coloured squares edged with lines of darker bricks makes a powerful design statement.

above right: The bracts of *Davidia involucrata* are a beautiful sight in late spring.

TIPS FOR L-SHAPED GARDENS

- Do not give in to the temptation to create two separate 'rooms' with the two legs of the L; it is more effective to link the areas together
- A specimen shrub or small statue at the far corner of the L will draw the eye and invite further exploration into the second part of the garden
- If the garden is laid to lawn, a small path going round the entire side would take the visitor to both parts
- Gardens with many angles often seem smaller than they are, so keep features small and pretty so that they do not overwhelm the space

CORNER GARDEN

The design for this corner plot uses the element of surprise provided by the two parts of the garden to full advantage, while at the same time linking them into a coherent whole. The focus is on the angled patio, while the other features and abundant planting ensure that there is plenty to enjoy throughout the garden.

PLANTING KEY

1 *Rosa* 'Salet'
2 *Rosa* 'Bride'
3 *Rosa* 'Paul Shirville'
4 *Rosa* 'Whisky Mac'
5 *Rosa* 'Golden Showers'
6 *Buxus microphylla*
7 *Rheum palmatum*
8 *Philadelphus* 'Dame Blanche'
9 *Aucuba japonica* f. *longifolia* 'Salicifolia'
10 *Helictotrichon sempervirens*
11 *Platycodon grandiflorus*
12 *Meconopsis betonicifolia*
13 *Bellis perennis* 'Pomponette'
14 *Rudbeckia hirta*
15 *Clematis* 'Miss Bateman'
16 *Centaurea cyanus*
17 *Calendula officinalis*
18 *Lavandula angustifolia* 'Hidcote'
19 *Echinops* 'Veitch's Blue'
20 *Rosa* 'Irish Eyes'
21 *Rosa* 'Atlantic Star'
22 *Jasminum officinale*
23 *Bergenia* 'Morgenröte'
24 *Campanula glomerata* 'Superba'
25 *Eryngium giganteum*
26 *Campanula lactiflora*
27 *Ligularia przewalskii*
28 *Rheum palmatum*
29 *Acer griseum*
30 *Lonicera fragrantissima*
31 *Hosta sieboldiana*
32 *Dryopteris filix-mas*
33 *Verbascum chaixii* 'Gainsborough'
34 *Mentha spicata*
35 *Sedum spectabile*
36 *Consolida ajacis*
37 *Delphinium* 'Mighty Atom'
38 *Digitalis purpurea*
39 *Malus* x *schiedeckeri* 'Red Jade'
40 *Helleborus orientalis*
41 *Buddleja davidii*
42 *Clematis* 'Trianon'
43 *Gladiolus* 'Columbine'
44 *Tropaeolum* 'Peach Melba'
45 *Veronica spicata*
46 *Lupinus arboreus*
47 *Hedera colchica*
48 *Magnolia stellata* 'Waterlily'
49 *Papaver orientale*

50 *Dianthus barbatus*
51 *Oenothera biennis*
52 *Eremurus stenophyllus*
53 *Hydrangea anomala* subsp. *petiolaris*
54 *Phlox paniculata* 'Sandringham'
55 *Astilbe* 'Peach Blossom'
56 *Artemisia absinthium*
57 *Philadelphus* 'Belle Etoile'
58 *Aruncus dioicus*
59 *Eucalyptus pauciflora* subsp. *niphophila*
60 *Ilex* x *altaclerensis* 'Golden King'
61 *Nepeta sibirica*
62 *Clematis* 'Jackmanii'
63 *Gentiana sino-ornata*
64 *Campsis radicans*
65 *Veronica gentianoides*
66 *Tagetes* 'Disco Golden Yellow'
67 *Stachys byzantina*
68 *Phlox paniculata* 'Orange Perfection'
69 *Jasminum nudiflorum*
70 *Kniphofia* 'Little Maid'
71 *Geranium dalmaticum*

72 *Dianthus* 'Pike's Pink'
73 *Thymus vulgaris*
74 *Helianthemum* 'The Bride'
75 *Aubrieta* 'Bressingham Pink'
76 *Saxifraga* 'Tumbling Waters'
77 *Lychnis alpina*
78 *Nymphaea odorata* (syn. *N.* 'Odorata Alba')
79 *Myriophyllum aquaticum*
80 *Stratiotes aloides*

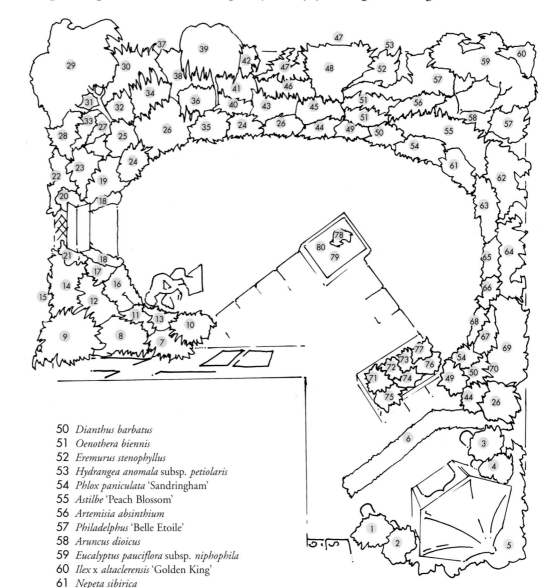

CORNER PLOTS ARE A CHALLENGE to the garden designer because they generally offer a larger than average amount of space yet incorporate a wide turn. The problem is how best to combine both parts of the garden and impose a feeling of unity on the entire area.

This garden uses the space to include something for everyone. There are lots of surprises, such as the seating area in the border and the statue, and there is a touch of formality in the rose garden. This contrasts with the lush green lawn, sweeping majestically around the house, which is, in turn, set against the sharply angled patio and raised beds, the gentle reflections of water and the pretty alpines. This is a garden to enjoy. It has places to sit, to eat, to play and to relax.

FEATURES

The two parts of the garden have been linked by the use of a sweeping lawn, and from either part of the garden it is obvious that it continues into the part that is not immediately visible. The second linking feature is the patio, which is set at an angle to the house. It is a pivotal point for the whole garden and sets the axis on the diagonal, which effectively ties the two parts together. It is meant to be seen, so large pavers have been used. It juts out into the lawn, creating a striking contrast in the central area of the garden.

Each part of this lovely garden has its own distinctive character, and attention is cleverly drawn to each one in different ways. The rose garden and gazebo offer a small formal area for where you can sit in peace and quiet. The raised alpine bed brings plants up to eye level and takes the eye across the garden to glimpse the flowerbeds on the far boundary.

The curved, sweeping character of the lawn makes use of the large area that is available and draws attention away from the sharp angles of the garden, leaving curvy flowerbeds, which are filled with scented and coloured plants that bring life and warmth to the plot.

Another secret seating area is a surprise: an informal seat from which the garden can be enjoyed. The overall impression of the garden is one of openness and space, and the lawn is deliberately kept clear of ornamentation because there is lots of interest all around this garden and the curve of the lawn is absolutely crucial to uniting the two parts of the garden.

The statue acts as a focal point, drawing the eye to this corner and thereby creating a long vista.

TIPS FOR CORNER GARDENS

- Avoid placing features in the centre of the lawn because these will make the garden appear like two 'rooms'
- If small trees are not to your liking, use statues in the far beds to attract they eye
- Disguise the boundaries as an effective way of losing the corner shape
- Keep weeds down to avoid competition

Although the pool and alpine beds are rectangular, they are set at angles to the garden so that they reflect each other and not the shape of the garden. They provide balance and two very different environments to extend the range of planting possibilities.

PLANTING

The ornamental trees break up the longest boundary, and their soft shapes and greenery will add peace and gentle movement to the garden.

In the borders lots of colours have been used to create warmth and vibrancy. Many differently shaped plants have been included to create a strongly shaped, deep boundary to the garden. The tall majestic spires of *Delphinium* 'Mighty Atom' and *Digitalis purpurea* (foxglove) contrast wonderfully with plants such as *Mentha spicata* (mint) and *Sedum spectabile*. Scented plants will release their fragrance, and visually striking plants like *Eryngium giganteum* add character. There are some architectural plants, such as *Magnolia stellata* 'Waterlily', and *Ilex* x *altaclerensis* 'Golden King' (holly) adds punctuation. Generally the planting is deep, encircling the garden to give total privacy and shelter.

Many of the plants in the garden have long seasons of interest. *Acer griseum* (paperbark maple), for example, has beautiful foliage and peeling bark. Plants with stunning but delicate flowers, like *Meconopsis betonicifolia* (Himalayan blue poppy) and *Platycodon grandiflorus* (balloon flower), contrast with the strong foliage interest of *Aucuba japonica* f. *longifolia* 'Salicifolia' and *Rheum palmatum*.

The shady corner is used to grow woodland plants and ferns, while the sunnier borders will be a blaze of colour in the summer months.

The entire boundary is clothed with climbing plants, forming a green background to the flowers and creating an enclosed, private feel.

opposite: The gazebo, set among formal clipped box, roses and tumbling climbers, offers a quiet and secluded spot in which to sit and enjoy the garden.

above: *Echinops ritro* 'Veitch's Blue' flowers more than once in each growing season.

SPLIT-LEVEL GARDEN

A basement courtyard can be transformed into a lively extension of the living space through the use of a clever split-level design. Raising the upper level maximizes the light received by the seating area – and the plants.

PLANTING KEY

1 *Aster amellus* 'King George'
2 *Chrysanthemum* 'Clara Curtis'
3 *Dahlia* Unwins Dwarf Group
4 *Sedum spectabile* 'Septemberglut' (syn. *S. spectabile* 'September Glow')
5 *Salvia officinalis* 'Aurea'
6 *Veronica longifolia* 'Blauriesin' (syn. *V. longifolia* 'Blue Giantess')
7 *Zantedeschia* 'Black Eyed Beauty'
8 *Hydrangea* 'Preziosa' (syn. *H. serrata* 'Preziosa')
9 *Camellia* 'Jean Pursel'
10 *Rosa rugosa* 'Rubra'
11 *Aster* x *frikartii* 'Flora's Delight'
12 *Rosa* 'Wendy Cussons'
13 *Aster* x *frikartii* 'Wunder von Stäfa' (syn. *A.* x *frikartii* 'Wonder of Stafa')
14 *Aucuba japonica* 'Hillieri'
15 *Euphorbia palustris*
16 *Hydrangea seemannii*
17 *Cotoneaster simonsii*
18 *Philodendron scandens*
19 *Elaeagnus* x *ebbingei* 'The Hague'
20 *Dicentra spectabilis*
21 *Thymus vulgaris*
22 *Geranium clarkei* 'Kashmir White'
23 *Cytisus battandieri*
24 *Achillea filipendulina*
25 *Lonicera periclymenum*
26 *Achillea ptarmica*
27 *Passiflora caerulea* 'Grandiflora'
28 *Fatsia japonica* 'Aurea'
29 *Pelargonium* 'Pixie Rose'
30 *Hypericum calycinum*
31 *Cistus monspeliensis*
32 *Iberis umbellata* Fairy Series
33 *Hypericum* 'Hidcote'
34 *Potentilla fruticosa* 'Princess' (syn. *P. fruticosa* 'Blink')
35 *Astilbe* 'Aphrodite'
36 *Hebe topiaria*
37 *Campanula lactiflora*
38 *Spiraea japonica* 'Goldflame'
39 *Fuchsia* 'Cascade'
40 *Canna* 'King Humbert'
41 *Iberis sempervirens* 'Weisser Zwerg' (syn. *I. sempervirens* 'Little Gem')
42 *Hedera nepalensis* var. *nepalensis* 'Suzanne' (syn. *H. helix* 'Suzanne')
43 *Rosa* 'Rosy Cushion' (syn. *R.* 'Interall')

44 *Dryopteris erythrosora*
45 *Photinia* x *fraseri* 'Red Robin'
46 *Clerodendrum thomasoniae*
47 *Myosotis sylvatica*
48 *Petunia* Duo Series
49 *Chaeonmeles speciosa* 'Falconnet Charlet'
50 *Euonymus fortunei* 'Emerald 'n' Gold'
51 *Lonicera fragrantissima*
52 *Pseudopanax lessonii* 'Gold Splash'
53 *Limnanthes douglasii*

54 *Foeniculum vulgare* 'Purpureum' (syn. *F. vulgare* 'Bronze')
55 *Aubrieta* x *cultorum* 'J.S. Baker'
56 *Aruncus dioicus* 'Kneiffii'
57 *Tiarella cordifolia*
58 *Daphne bholua* 'Jaqueline Postill'
59 *Choisya ternata*
60 *Salvia officinalis* 'Tricolor'
61 *Parthenocissus henryana* (syn. *Vitis henryana*)
62 *Brachyglottis greyi* (syn. *Senecio greyi*)
63 *Tropaeolum tricolor* (syn. *T. tricolorum*)

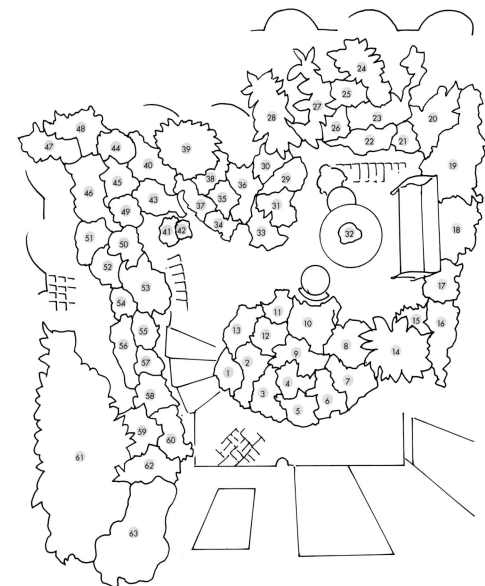

SPLIT-LEVEL GARDEN

MANY OLDER HOUSES HAVE a garden that is accessed from a basement later re-modelled in order to allow more light into the kitchen or dining area. This garden is designed on two levels to cope with such an arrangement. The levels are asymmetrical and joined by steps, the shape of which echoes the curved retaining wall of a raised bed.

The garden is overlooked from two sides and is also below street level and very shaded. The clever design raises the main area of the garden towards the light, while still offering shelter and seclusion. The plants themselves link both parts of the garden, as does the use of the same bricks, but attention is focused on the upper, roomy level and the vibrant, rich planting.

The lower area of this garden is too small to be used for seating and is in constant shade, so very few plants will thrive there. However, plants from the upper levels are encouraged to cascade down, providing colour and interest as well as improving the view from the window. The eye is drawn to the upper level by the clever use of the furniture, water basin and plants.

FEATURES

This is a square plot and because it is surrounded by high walls it has the potential to be dull and boring, especially as the lower level is shaded and very small. The asymmetrical design minimizes the square feel and introduces different depths for variety and interest. The dominating end wall has been lightened with a colour wash and cloaked with lots of climbing plants. White trellis, with curved, attractive shapes along the top, further softens the wall and provides a framework for the shade-tolerant climbers. It encourages the eye to travel upwards to space and light. The water basin is an eyecatching feature, which draws the eye to the far corner, where it nestles among long-flowering plants, such as campanula and roses.

Raised beds bring the plants nearer the light and gently lift the eye-line, reducing the

impact of the difference in levels. The shapes of the beds are not, in this garden, totally disguised by plants because allowing their shape and lines to be seen detracts from the strong, square shape of the plot and draws attention to the curving, unusual lines of the beds, making the garden much more interesting.

Uniformity and continuity are provided by using the same bricks for both areas, but arranging them in a different pattern emphasizes the different character of the two areas. The walls of the raised beds are built of the same bricks to unite the entire garden.

The seating area is surrounded entirely by greenery, creating a secluded haven to relax and entertain in. Here, the harsh edges of the brickwork are softened by trailing plants that spill out on to the floor, bringing the plants into every part of the area and subtly dividing it from the rest of the garden. The furniture is white to complement the trellis, and the white walls of the house, together with the trellis and furniture, reflect sunlight and lighten the feel to this garden, which could otherwise be shady and dull.

The eye is drawn to the upper level by the central bed and steps, then on to the plants and asymmetrical beds of the upper level and then higher still to the trellis and plants there, so creating a sense of space and an attractive, sheltered garden.

In the lower area a single container is used to disguise the hard angle where the two walls join.

PLANTING

Largely in shades of pink and red, the plants have been carefully selected to reinforce the strong design. The central raised bed is packed with colourful flowering shrubs and trailing plants to link the two areas, and this is an excellent way of getting colour into the lower area without constructing more beds or using containers that will take up space.

Tropaeolum tricolor (nasturtium) is grown up the wall to bring the planting closer to the house and complete the transformation into

another room, an extension of the living area.

Hanging baskets filled with seasonal and evergreen plants add depth to the trellis and further break up the wall. Using baskets of different sizes broadens the range of plants you can grow and makes it possible for those that need to be in full sun to be placed in the appropriate positions.

TIPS FOR SPLIT-LEVEL GARDENS

- Draw the eye upwards with colourful plants in hanging baskets with trailing plants to add depth to the foliage
- Keep beds neat and tidy so that they do not look cluttered
- Make sure that the trellis is strong enough to hold the weight of all the hanging baskets and climbers
- Include focal plants in the borders to attract the eye

opposite: A split-level garden, the different levels unified by the use of similar bricks and colour-themed planting throughout.

above left: Hanging baskets suspended from trellis encourage the eye upwards and break up the wall with bright seasonal colour.

above: Twining plants like this *Passiflora caerulea* (passion flower) allow parts of a white wall to peep through painted trellis for a softening effect.

FORMAL POOL GARDEN

A pair of small, square pools, a simple expanse of cream-coloured paving and rich yet uncomplicated planting are the elements that ensure this unusual design really works. A pool statue draws the eye to the more densely planted far end of the garden, while close to the house the feel is light and airy.

PLANTING KEY

1   Clematis 'Royalty'
2   Rosa 'Emily Gray'
3   Phalaris arundinacea var. picta
4   Dianthus 'Pierrot'
5   Lavandula angustifolia 'Jean Davis'
6   Potentilla 'Gibson's Scarlet'
7   Thunbergia coccinea
8   Campanula isophylla 'Alba'
9   Primula bulleyana
10 Armeria maritima 'Bloodstone'
11 Saxifraga 'Clarence Elliott' (syn. S. umbrosa var. primuloides 'Elliot's Variety')
12 Hemerocallis 'Dido'
13 Spiraea japonica 'Allgold'
14 Anemone hupehensis
15 Butomus umbellatus
16 Sagittaria japonica
17 Ranunculus aquatilis
18 Typha minima
19 Hosta undulata var. undulata (syn. H. 'Mediovariegata')
20 Cordateria argentea
21 Epimedium grandiflorum
22 Adiantum formosum
23 Vinca minor 'Bowles' Variety'
24 Anaphalis triplinervis
25 Helleborus argutifolius (syn. H. corsicus)
26 Arbutus unedo
27 Ajuga pyramidalis
28 Bouteloua gracilis (syn. B. oligostachys)
29 Phalaris arundinacea
30 Houttuynia cordata 'Chameleon'
31 Myosotis sylvatica 'Ultramarine'
32 Iris laevigata 'Variegata'
33 Iris pseudacorus 'Golden Fleece'
34 Nymphaea 'Odorata Turicensis'
35 Hosta 'Sum and Substance'
36 Luzula sylvatica 'Marginata' (syn. L. sylvatica 'Aureomarginata')
37 Persicaria affinis 'Darjeeling Red'
38 Polemonium 'Lambrook Mauve'
39 Kirengeshoma palmata
40 Carpinus betulus
41 Ajuga reptans 'Atropururea' (syn. A. reptans 'Purpurea')
42 Hyssopus officinalis
43 Fothergilla major
44 Helleborus odorus
45 Fritillaria affinis

46 x Fatshedera lizei 'Pia'
47 Euphorbia dulcis 'Chameleon'
48 Heuchera 'Scintillation'
49 Geranium pratense 'Plenum Violaceum' (syn. G. pratense 'Plenum Purpureum')
50 Pyrus salicifolia 'Pendula'
51 Epilobium angustifolium var. album
52 Hemerocallis 'Edna Spalding'
53 Daphne pontica
54 Clematis 'Lasurstern'
55 Rosa 'Alister Stella Gray'
56 Impatiens 'Blackberry Ice'

57 Sedum spectabile
58 Dieffenbachia seguine 'Memoria Corsii'
59 Daphne x manteniana 'Manten'
60 Geranium pratense 'Mrs Kendall Clark'
61 Helichrysum splendidum (syn. H. alveolatum)
62 Ruta graveolens 'Jackman's Blue'
63 Salvia lavandulifolia
64 Eucryphia x nymansensis
65 Euonymus fortunei 'Emerald Cushion'
66 Elaeagnus pungens 'Goldrim'
67 Rhus typhina

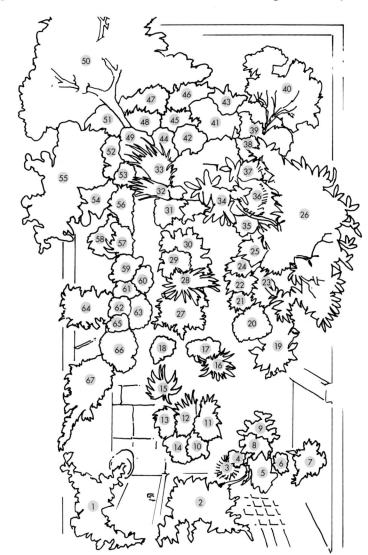

FORMAL POOL GARDEN

REFLECTION AND GEOMETRICAL precision are the key elements in this garden. The inclusion of two small pools, which mirror each other in shape and size, provides a relatively large surface area of water without dominating the garden, as a larger, single pool would do. Although softened a little by plants, the formal rectangular lines are maintained throughout the plot.

This garden breaks a lot of rules, suggesting that it has a slightly maverick owner. It has been designed as if it were bigger than it really is, but the design works. Usually, for example, small pavers look best in small areas, but here the effect of using the large, cream-coloured paving stones is to make the garden appear larger and lighter.

The plants are uncomplicated, and varieties have been chosen that prefer shady, moist conditions. Shades of red and greens in the foliage echo the hues of the water and the brickwork. With its very strong design, clear lines and rich, varied planting, this garden is one that invites you to explore it.

FEATURES

The large, rectangular, cream-coloured pavers reflect light and emphasize the clean lines and regularity of the design. The main focal points are the two square pools, and little in the garden detracts from them, ensuring that the formal feel is maintained. The pools reflect the sky above and the foliage around them, adding another dimension to the garden, and the pools themselves offer a different medium and extend the range of planting that is possible.

The garden is subtly divided into two halves. The area nearer the house is very light and airy, with the hard lines of the pavers and pool deliberately maintained. In the other half of the garden, further from the house, there is a narrow flowerbed on one side and a wider bed on the other, which has space for a range of plants that cannot be grown in the part of the garden nearer to the house

A single statue at the far end of the pool

furthest from the house serves as a focal point, drawing the eye down the garden, and the trickling water from the pot adds sound and another dimension to the garden.

The brick walls, which provide a strong contrast to the pavers, are an effective backdrop to the planting, but the house walls are painted white in order to reflect light back into the garden.

A double row of bricks in front of the far bed introduces a change of surface, and a few pots containing small shrubs in front of the bed give added depth to the plants and make the garden seem larger. The use of a square

container in the group between the pools emphasizes the shape of the pools but breaks the continuity by adding some evergreen plants with interesting foliage.

PLANTING

The planting is as diverse as would normally be associated with a larger garden, and the inclusion of the trees is important in maintaining the illusion of space. The two small trees, *Carpinus betulus* (hornbeam) and *Pyrus salicifolia* 'Pendula' (weeping pear), not only add height but also serve to cover the bare walls effectively.

The trees are balanced by areas of interest at lower levels in the garden. Using plants of diverse habits and heights provides lots of variety, and the eye is drawn to many places in the garden without the clear geometrical pattern being interrupted.

In the portion of the garden near to the house the walls are largely bare, but they are increasingly clothed with plants until, in the far corners, they are almost totally covered, creating the illusion that the garden goes on further than it does.

The planting around the pools is simple, with a few overhanging plants at the edges so that their strong outlines are uninterrupted.

Colours are kept gentle, and a large, cream-coloured, earthenware planter holds a variety of pink and purple flowering plants to bring colour closer to the house. Containers are also used to bring plants to areas that would otherwise be bare, thus limiting the need to create flowerbeds and allowing the continuity of the paving to be maintained, and one or two small ornamental trees in containers can be moved to give the best effect at different seasons.

The trellis against the house gives extra room for climbers and increases the surface on which plants can grow without taking any space from the garden itself.

TIPS FOR FORMAL POOL GARDENS

- Point between the pavers, leaving no gaps and no places for weeds to get a hold
- Keep pavers moss free and non-slip
- Include plants that like shady conditions and that have subtle flowers
- Plants lots of evergreens to maintain interest high throughout the year
- Use a flexible butyl liner for the pools
- Select water plants carefully, because achieving and maintaining a balance and controlling the growth of algae in a small pool is harder that in a large one
- In a very small garden a bubble or millstone fountain or a container pool could be a suitable alternative
- Top up pool levels in summer by trickling in tapwater

opposite: In this formal pool garden, rectangles, squares and straight lines predominate, linking the paving, pebbles, seating and pools.

above left: Clematis and roses can be grown together on house and garden walls to provide extra flower power without taking up valuable space.

above: This pool statue, surrounded by the lush foliage and cool white flowers of *Zantedeschia aethiopica* (arum lily), provides a striking focal point and the added attractions of moving water and sound.

SEMI-FORMAL POOL GARDEN

Two distinctive formal pools, herringbone brickwork and an unusual curving path, plus a rich diversity of foliage and flowers, have transformed this once dull rectangular plot into something really special. A spacious seating area close to the house makes it easy to enjoy the garden at any time.

PLANTING KEY

1 *Hydrangea aspera*
2 *Hebe* 'Mrs Winder' (syn. *H.* 'Waikiki', *H.* 'Warleyensis)
3 *Daphne* x *burkwoodii* 'Astrid'
4 *Veronica spicata* subsp. *spicata*
5 *Buddleja davidii* 'Royal Red'
6 *Deutzia monbeigii*
7 *Hosta* 'So Sweet'
8 *Hydrangea macrophylla* 'Ayesha'
9 *Campsis radicans*
10 *Sarcococca hookeriana* var. *digyna* 'Purple Stern'
11 *Mahonia lomariifolia*
12 *Cornus alba* 'Elegantissima'
13 *Hydrangea* 'Preziosa' (syn. *H. serrata* 'Preziosa')
14 *Sambucus racemosa* 'Plumosa Aurea'
15 *Browallia speciosa* 'White Troll'
16 *Olearia albida*
17 *Yucca filamentosa* 'Bright Edge'
18 *Lavandula angustifolia* 'Hidcote' (syn. *L.* 'Hidcote Blue')
19 *Brachyglottis greyi* (syn. *Senecio greyi*)
20 *Iris pseudacorus*
21 *Typha minima*
22 *Iris ensata* 'Blue Peter'
23 *Lysichiton americanus*
24 *Populus alba* 'Raket'
25 *Thymus* x *citriodorus* 'Bertram Anderson'
26 *Pittosporum tenuifolium* 'Deborah'
27 *Yucca gloriosa*
28 *Skimmia japonica* 'Nymans'
29 *Eriobotrya japonica*
30 *Lavatera* 'Shorty'
31 *Deutzia scabra* 'Candidissima'
32 *Buddleja globosa*
33 *Hedera helix* 'Glacier'
34 *Actinidia kolomikta*
35 *Elaeagnus pungens* 'Dicksonii'
36 *Phormium tenax* 'Aurora'
37 *Phormium* 'Maori Chief' (syn. *P.* 'Rainbow Chief')
38 *Spiraea* 'Arguta' (syn. *S.* x *arguta* 'Bridal Wreath')
39 *Pelargonium* 'Robe'
40 *Pelargonium* 'Rica'
41 *Eschscholzia californica* 'Monarch Art Shades'
42 *Blechnum spicant*
43 *Erythronium revolutum*
44 *Hemerocallis* 'Dido'
45 *Doryanthes palmeri*
46 *Iris sibirica* 'Mountain Lake'
47 *Pontederia cordata*
48 *Hydrocharis morsus-rannae*
49 *Butomus umbellatus*
50 *Caltha palustris*
51 *Escallonia rubra* 'Woodside' (syn. *E. rubra* 'Pygmaea')
52 *Fritillaria imperialis*
53 *Hosta* 'Tall Boy'
54 *Elaeagnus* x *ebbingei* 'Gilt Edge'
55 *Desmodium elegans* (syn. *D. tiliifolium*)

42, 43 and 44 underplanted around taller plants

THIS GARDEN IS CENTRED AROUND two pools, which are divided by a curving brick path and a bog garden. Having pools and a bog garden greatly extends the range of plants that can be grown and creates an attractive habitat for wildlife. Because of the rich diversity of plants there is a huge variety of textures and shapes, and despite the path that winds through the garden, the space feels positively enveloped by a cloak of greenery, making it a secluded hideaway from the neighbouring gardens.

Simplicity is the key to the success of the design, which is mirrored along a horizontal axis, with the shed complementing the shape of the steps and the pools mirroring each other. The gentle colours of the water are reflected in the foliage – calm greens, blues and greys are found among areas of lush greens. This is a garden that you will want to step into and explore. A small fountain combines movement and stillness to make a garden that is inviting and relaxing.

FEATURES
The brick path extends from the house to the small brick shed in the far corner of the garden. In the sitting area the weathered bricks are laid herringbone-style, while the area beyond the first pool has been paved with straight small bricks. The stone slabs used as coping flow from one half to the other to tie the two areas together. The shallow step between the pools creates a subtle change of level without being dramatic and encourages visitors to pause to admire the plants.

The stillness of the water in the pools adds charm to the garden and reinforces the strong design. The water, reflecting both sky and foliage, will complement and emphasize the business of leaf movement and insect life in the garden.

A small raised bed in front of the shed elevates several small shrubs, which provide an effective screen in front of the structure, and the bed continues along the far side of the farther pool, offering additional space to grow a variety of stunning plants.

The brick walls have been painted white to create a bright, sunny garden and also to provide a good background against which the planting can be admired. Trellis is used on top of the three garden walls to increase the height without reducing light and to provide an extension of the growing area for plants. The wood of the trellis and of the steps leading to the sitting area is picked up by the table and chairs.

PLANTING

A huge range of plants has been used, but there is still plenty of room for a spacious area for sitting out because most of the planting is contained in beds at the bottom of the walls, leaving the central area clear and the shapes of the hard landscaping obvious. The beds allow the planting to continue unbroken all round the garden for seclusion and privacy. Architectural plants, such as *Phormium tenax* 'Aurora', *P.* 'Maori Chief' and *Doryanthes palmeri* (spear lily), create focal points and add a range of heights but the main focus remains within the garden itself.

The clear edges of the pools at the path side, uncluttered by overhanging plants, emphasize the formality of the pools, which is, at the same time, offset by a diverse range of floating aquatic plants. Both pools have a lush background of plants, and a wide variety of foliage forms has been used to create diversity and interest. The miniature elegance of *Typha minima* (reedmace) and *Iris ensata* 'Blue Peter', backed by the strong architec-

tural spikes of *Yucca filamentosa* 'Bright Edge', create a stunning effect at this point. *Populus alba* 'Raket' (poplar) adds rustling grey foliage to the barer part of the boundary.

A bog garden offers the opportunity to grow plants particularly suited to this damp ground. Such an area is easily created by extending the pool liner into a depression, which can be filled with good quality soil.

Many of the aquatic plants are planted in containers to reduce their spread and maintenance. Once the balance of plant and insect life is established the pools should be self-sustaining and the water should remain clear, although regular checks for pests and weeds, such as blanketweed and pondweed, need to be kept up. Always remove any leaves that fall into the pool to prevent a build up of toxic gases released by the decaying process.

opposite: The curving brick path creates a dynamic division between the two formal pools, which are surrounded by plantings emphasizing foliage and form.

above left: *Iris pseudacorus* is a superb plant for a formal pool, its upright form and sword-shaped leaves the perfect complement to stiff stems of clear yellow flowers.

above: A bog garden affords the opportunity to grow a wide range of moisture-loving plants with lush, attractive foliage and pretty flowers.

TIPS FOR SEMI-FORMAL POOL GARDENS

- Keep paths clean and clear and point between bricks to suppress weeds
- Keep the water clear and free of weeds and algae
- Trim back plants that trail in the water
- Keep rampant plants in containers to limit their spread so that pools do not become overgrown

PLANT ENTHUSIAST'S GARDEN

This garden is crammed with plants – trees and shrubs, roses and climbers, perennials and grasses, alpines and annuals – but to work as a whole, the different features and habitats linked in a harmonious picture.

PLANTING KEY

1 *Rosa* 'Paul's Scarlet Climber'
2 *Rosa banksiae*
3 *Buxus microphylla*
4 *Aubrieta* x *cultorum*
5 *Cortaderia selloana*
6 *Carex oshimensis* 'Evergold'
7 *Stipa gigantea*
8 *Fargesia nitida*
9 *Festuca glauca* 'Elijah Blue'
10 *Phalaris arundinacea* 'Picta'
11 *Yucca gloriosa*
12 *Phormium* 'Bronze Beauty'
13 *Hakonechloa macra* 'Aureola'
14 *Agave parviflora*
15 *Phormium* 'Sundowner'
16 *Buddleja globosa*
17 *Genista lydia*
18 *Hamamelis* x *intermedia* 'Allgold'
19 *Corylus avellana* 'Contorta'
20 *Malus floribunda*
21 *Magnolia campbellii* 'Charles Raffill'
22 Cordon apples and pears
23 *Cornus alba* 'Elegantissima'
24 *Cornus alba* 'Siberica'
25 *Campsis* x *tagliabuana* 'Madame Galen'
26 *Ipomoea indica*
27 *Dryopteris affinis* 'Crispa Gracilis'
28 *Matteuccia struthiopteris*
29 *Euphorbia amygdaloides* 'Purpurea' (syn. *E. amygdaloides* 'Rubra')
30 *Ligularia* 'The Rocket'
31 *Hosta fortunei*
32 *Cyclamen hederifolium*
32 *Prunus pendula* 'Pendula Rosea' (syn. *P.* x *subhirtella* 'Pendula')
34 *Hibiscus syriacus*
35 *Paeonia lactiflora*
36 *Potentilla fruticosa* 'Elizabeth'
37 *Potentilla fruticosa* var. *dahurica* 'Farrer's White'
38 *Lobelia* 'Queen Victoria'
39 *Lunaria annua* 'Variegata'
40 *Physostegia virginiana*
41 *Clematis* 'Jackmanii Rubra'
42 *Delphinium* 'Tessa' mixed with *Gladiolus* cultivars
43 *Eryngium alpinum* 'Amethyst'
44 *Papaver orientale*
45 *Eryngium maritimum*
46 *Nepeta sibirica*

47 *Geranium* 'Johnson's Blue'
48 *Helichrysum italicum*
49 *Mimulus lewisii*
50 *Geranium psilostemon*
51 *Philadelphus* 'Belle Etoile'
52 *Akebia quinata*
53 *Bougainvillea* 'San Diego Red' syn. *B.* 'Scarlett O'Hara'
54 *Eccremocarpus scaber*
55 *Verbena* 'Silver Anne'
56 *Nigella damascena* 'Miss Jekyll'
57 *Antirrhinum majus*

58 *Tagetes* 'Disco Golden Yellow'
59 *Lobularia maritima*
60 *Cosmos bipinnatus* 'Sea Shells'
61 *Nicotiana sylvestris*
62 *Iberis umbellata*
63 *Centaurea cyanus*
64 *Clarkia amoena*
65 *Myosotis sylvatica* 'Music'
66 *Petunia* Grandiflora cultivars
67 *Rosa* 'Invincible'
68 *Rosa* 'Sunset Boulevard'
69 *Rosa* 'Iceberg'

70 *Rosa* 'Freedom'
71 *Rosa* 'Fascination'
72 *Rosa* 'Bride'
73 *Rosa* 'Tintinara'
74 *Rosa* 'Awareness'
75 *Armeria maritima*
76 *Artemisia stelleriana* 'Nana'
77 *Sempervivum tectorum*
78 *Aurinia saxatilis* (syn. *Alyssum saxatile*)
79 *Primula* 'Wanda'
80 *Dianthus deltoides*

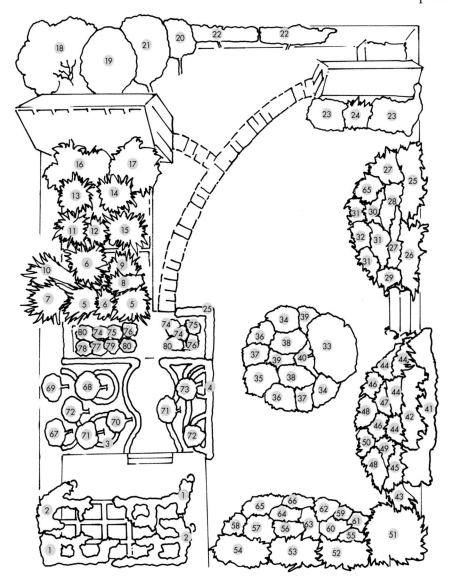

THE DESIGN HERE HAS BEEN carefully thought out to offer the plant enthusiast the greatest number of different habitats in order to grow the widest possible range of plants within a fairly limited area. The design also ensures that the plant enthusiast has a garden that is full of character and interest but is balanced and linked together.

Plants from many groups can be found, from poppies to roses, and from climbers to grasses. Every conceivable space has been filled with interesting and diverse plants, making this a plant lover's idea of heaven.

There is always something to do amid the ever-changing planting, and the enthusiast will be able to indulge their passion all year round. The small areas of different garden styles enable the keen gardener to grow many speciality plants and show them off. A lot of small areas can look cluttered and mismatched, but this clever design links everything together.

The garden will need attention all year round, and some of the tender plants will have to be moved into the greenhouse in winter, but for a plant enthusiast this should

not be a problem. In any high-maintenance garden doing little often will prevent the jobs from piling up and becoming overwhelming.

FEATURES

The main attraction in this garden is the planting, and the design is intended to create the perfect places to show off the plants. A pergola projects out from the house, creating a shady seating area on the patio. Cloaked in a selection of climbing plants, it offers privacy and shelter from the sun. From the pergola the garden can be seen through the roses and the gentle scents of the plants appreciated in the air.

In front of this area is the rose garden, which is covered with gravel. The hybrid teas and floribundas are planted among a clipped box hedge, which forms a miniature knot garden. The path is of small, unobtrusive, grey-tinged pavers.

Different coloured gravel makes a bold statement against which grasses, such as *Festuca glauca* 'Elijah Blue', *Phalaris arundinacea* 'Picta' (gardener's garters) and *Hakonechloa macra* 'Aureola', together with *Yucca gloriosa*, *Phormium* 'Bronze Beauty' and other specimen plants can be seen to best effect. Scree will show up well against the red bricks, focusing the eye on it; the grasses will be set off perfectly by the yellow gravel.

The greenhouse is sited in a position where it will get the best light, and although it is partially hidden by the wall it is very easily accessible.

PLANTING

Annuals are grown in the bed close to the house. These can be changed seasonally and offer a chance to grow favourite plants in a sheltered site.

The colours of the flowers have been chosen to blend together to create a gentle, harmonious feel, except for the main flowerbed, which is packed with plants in bright, bold colours to create a 'hot' bed. The vivid and warm shades of *Papaver orientale* (oriental

tures, which are blended together to give flow and movement to the shape of the beds. Some of the plants have quite heart-stopping beauty and form, such as *Eryngium alpinum* 'Amethyst', with its spiky, sharp leaves and wonderful blue flowers, and *Lunaria annua* 'Variegata', with its characteristic desiccated oval seedpods.

The back of the garden is planted with a range of shrubs, and near the shed are some fruit trees, which will produce a fine harvest in late summer.

The shady area under the overhanging branches of the neighbour's tree is damp, but it is the perfect place to grow ferns, hostas and other shade-loving species. Woodland species are grown here for interest and seasonal colour, too.

The raised island bed lifts the eye-line and hides some of the rest of the garden, immediately arousing interest because it is clear that there is more, unseen garden beyond. The island bed itself is the perfect place for a rock garden and alpines, and alpines grown in scree beds provide colour and interest all year round.

poppy) draw the eye, while among the interesting climbers are *Akebia quinata* (chocolate vine) and *Bougainvillea* 'San Diego Red'. More climbers are grown on the trellis beside the garden shed.

A wonderful side-effect of having many different plants in a garden is that there is automatically a wide range of forms and tex-

opposite: A pergola offers the opportunity to grow a mixed range of climbers for both foliage and flowers – and, above a seating area like this, scent as well.

above: The climber *Akebia quinata* is a real enthusiast's plant, producing clusters of flowers that are unusual in both colour and form.

above right: A sharply drained raised bed is the ideal spot for a collection of alpines, shown off to advantage against the mulch of gravel chippings.

TIPS FOR PLANT ENTHUSIASTS' GARDENS

- Always purchase good quality plants so they grow well and become good plants for display and propagation
- Keep the lawn well maintained so that the lush green grass offers a solid background against which plants can be seen to best effect – the eye should go to the plants, not the holes in the lawn
- Install an irrigation system, such as a trickle or drip feed arrangement, for wide, inaccessible borders, although small areas that require less water can be watered from a watering can
- Make sure you know how to care for each group of plants
- Move container-grown specimens around to display them at their best at different times of the year
- Keep surfaces clear and clean to maintain their use as backgrounds against which to show off the plants

JAPANESE-STYLE GARDEN

This garden is all about shape and form, contrast and complement, drawn into a unified whole through repetition and geometry. The strong design links together individual areas, materials and plants to create a pervading ambience of calm and tranquillity.

PLANTING KEY

1 *Lavandula angustifolia* 'Hidcote' (syn. *L.* 'Hidcote Blue')
2 *Lilium candidum*
3 *Nepeta sibirica* (syn. *N. macrantha*)
4 *Hemerocallis* 'Apple Tart'
5 *Acer negundo* 'Variegatum' (syn. *A. negundo* 'Argenteovariegatum')
6 *Hebe pinguifolia* 'Pagei'
7 *Festuca eskia*
8 *Festuca glauca* 'Elijah Blue'
9 *Phyllostachys nigra*
10 *Humulus lupulus*
11 *Ruta graveolens*
12 *Clematis* 'William Kennett'
13 *Senecio cineraria* 'White Diamond'
14 *Kniphofia triangularis* subsp. *triangularis* (syn. *K. galpinii*)
15 *Veronica austriaca* subsp. *teucrium* 'Crater Lake Blue'
16 *Macleaya* x *kewensis*
17 *Hedera helix* 'Eva' (syn. *H. helix* 'Liz')
18 *Hydrangea macrophylla* 'Madame Emile Mouillère'
19 *Sasa veitchii* (syn. *Arundinaria veitchii*)
20 *Ficus pumila* 'Minima'
21 *Robinia hispida* 'Rosea'
22 *Clematis* 'Nelly Moser'
23 *Buxus microphylla* 'Green Pillow'
24 *Buxus sempervirens* 'Elegantissima'
25 *Phormium* 'Dazzler'
26 *Orbea variegata* (syn. *Stapelia variegata*)
27 *Oxalis* 'Ione Hecker'
28 *Dianthus* 'La Bourboule'
29 *Berberis thunbergii* 'Bagatelle'
30 *Prunus* 'Accolade'
31 *Gleditsia triacanthos* 'Sunburst'
32 *Rhododendron yakushimanum*
33 *Tanacetum ptarmiciflorum* (syn. *Pyrethrum ptarmiciflorum*)
34 *Lamium maculatum* 'Beacon Silver'
35 *Celmisia ramulosa*
36 *Papaver orientale* 'Allegro'
37 *Artemisia* 'Powis Castle'
38 *Pyracantha* 'Golden Charmer'
39 *Tradescantia pallida* 'Purpurea'
40 *Lobularia maritima* 'Snow Crystals'
41 *Quercus robur* (bonsai)
42 *Cerastium tomentosum*
43 *Alnus incana* (bonsai)

44 *Lithops marmorata*
45 *Yucca gloriosa*
46 *Crassula ovata*
47 *Clematis montana* var. *rubens* 'Elizabeth'

48 *Hosta fortunei* var. *albopicta* (syn. *H.* 'Aureomaculata')
49 *Dianthus* 'Joanne'
50 *Erigeron* 'Gaiety'

Japanese-Style Garden

The main design feature of this garden is the geometric layout of the floor, and several different materials have been used to create patterns of wood, bricks, gravel and stone. Water, light and a few carefully chosen feature plants are then used to contrast with and complement this geometric pattern. It is not only the different surfaces that give each area its distinctive character, however, but the ways in which they are laid out. The brick, wood and gravel will look subtly different in wet or dry weather.

The unity and small scale of the design mean that materials can be combined to appear natural and harmonious, but the scheme also makes it possible to include greater variety in a small area. An individual and strong design statement, this garden offers quiet sanctuary and peace. It has an uncluttered feel yet contains many elements that are united and tied together.

Strong design, using visually striking hard landscaping, is traditional in Eastern gardens and is used here to great effect. Every single feature and plant has earned its place and is carefully chosen and sited. Every element is important and forms a focal point in its own right. The garden has drama, character and individuality and suggests a strong, calm personality.

FEATURES

While Western gardens concentrate on introducing curves to create a relaxed feel, in an Eastern garden it is the configuration of geometrical patterns in precise and ordered arrangements that creates an harmonious space. Many small areas, each contrasting with its neighbours, are created within the garden. As important as the features is the space between them, and the placing of individual plants and artefacts is crucial to the overall scheme. Nothing is complicated, and the simplicity and clean lines add to the sense of care and search for perfection.

The patio is laid in a symmetrical pattern of bricks and has a few plants in containers.

The pots contain seasonal plants and there is a stunning *Phormium* 'Dazzler' as a focal point at the end of the garden. The L-shaped pool around the seating area is crossed by two simple wooden bridges, which neatly take you into other areas. A pump feeds water into the canal, and the small change in level produces a gentle waterfall. The water acts like a mirror, reflecting and bringing movement and light into the garden.

The interplay of materials is emphasized by using timber slats set in a base of gravel to contrast with the brickwork and fencing in a series of geometric shapes. The gravel is largely bare, except for a few carefully placed,

interesting plants, and the small tree will provide shade in this sunny area.

This area is linked to the neighbouring shady area by the wooden slats and a line of bricks set in the gravel. A tiny arbour, created in a covered pergola, is set against the wall. A short flight of steps leads into another shady area, which is both defined and linked to the patio by the use of the same bricks, and another simple wooden bridge takes you back to the seating area, completing the unity of the garden. There are no loose ends: absolutely everything is linked and tied together, making the garden a place of peace and harmony.

The tall bamboo screen adds to the oriental feel, and a stone statue has been chosen for its form to add to the composition.

The furniture is limited to a table and chairs on the spacious patio and to a bench tucked away inside the covered pergola.

PLANTING

In keeping with the ambience created by the hard landscaping, the planting is simple but carefully chosen and positioned. To create an Eastern feel, hardy but exotic-looking plants in pots are used. A few well-placed, strong, spiky plants will give an impression of coming from faraway places.

The shape and form of the plants is as important as those of the features. A single ivy climbs the fence to provide a subtle green backdrop, but the wooden fencing is kept largely bare to allow the wood to be appreciated for its natural beauty and subtly lend its properties to the garden.

A few containers are used to take plants into areas where they are needed. A single container on a square stone against the wall provides a small focal point. Low shrubs backed with climbers add richness to the shaded part of the garden, and the rectangular beds in front of the fence complement the shapes of the bridges and wooden slats.

opposite: In this simple water feature, the pebble-filled square stone set in the centre of the bowl echoes the smooth stones and paving slabs used on the surrounding gravel area.

left: Timber slats set in a gravel base provide a contrast of texture, colour and material. Low-growing carpeting plants are allowed to creep just over the edge of the wood.

above: *Phormium* 'Sundowner' and *Arctotis* 'Flame' are both striking plants and together they make a stunning focal point.

TIPS FOR JAPANESE-STYLE GARDENS

- Lanterns, piles of rock and deer scarers are traditional ornaments and can be bought from garden centres and specialist companies to create an authentic atmosphere
- Use plants with strong shapes and move them around until you are happy with their positions
- Study illustrations of Japanese gardens in books and magazines for inspiration and guidance on planting and positioning ornaments

CHILDREN'S GARDEN

A sunken sandpit, Wendy house, swing and slide, birdtable and birdbath – there are plenty of safe and practical features in this garden to keep children happily occupied for hours. Including an area in which they can grow their own vegetables and flowers will encourage them to become gardeners themselves.

PLANTING KEY

1   *Petroselinum crispum* (parsley)
2   *Origanum onites* (oregano)
3   *Mentha spicata* (spearmint)
4   *Thymus vulgaris* (thyme)
5   *Allium schoenoprasum* (chives)
6   *Salvia officinalis* (sage)
7   Strawberry 'Ostara'
8   Strawberry 'Domanil'
9   *Clematis* 'Etoile Rose'
10 *Clematis montana* var. *rubens* 'Tetrarose'
11 *Solanum crispum*
12 *Ceanothus* x *delileanus*
13 *Syringa vulgaris*
14 *Fagus sylvatica*
15 *Pyrus communis* 'Onward'
16 *Prunus domestica* 'Anna Späth'
17 *Malus domestica* 'Royal Gala'
18 *Lonicera periclymenum*
19 *Buddleja globosa*
20 *Iberis sempervirens*
21 *Lathyrus odoratus*
22 *Helianthus annuus*
23 *Tulipa* 'Purissima'
24 *Tulipa* 'Page Polka'
25 *Jasminum officinale*
26 *Hydrangea anomala* subsp. *petiolaris*
27 *Actinidia kolomikta*
28 *Lonicera fragrantissima*
29 *Erica arborea* var. *alpina*
30 *Erica carnea* 'March Seedling'
31 *Erica carnea* 'December Red'
32 *Erica vagans* 'Fiddlestone'
33 *Calluna vulgaris* 'Finale'
34 *Calluna vulgaris* 'Oxshott Common'
35 *Erica cinerea* 'Purple Beauty'
36 *Erica vagans* 'Saint Keverne'
37 *Jasminum nudiflorum*

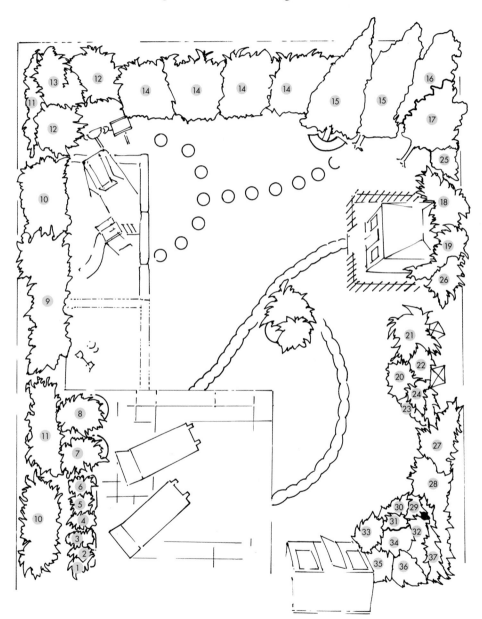

cycles, sit and relax or play. The sunken sand-pit has a 25cm (10in) wall built around it to contain the sand, and it is close enough to the house and patio for the children to be in view when they are playing in it. Later, when the children have grown out of it, the sandpit can easily be converted into a water feature because a pit has been excavated under it, which will later house an electric pump to operate a small fountain, and the pool can be readily installed, already complete with a surrounding wall.

The patio area itself is made from uniform, square paving slabs in two contrasting colours. The advantage of using stones in a regular pattern is that four slabs can be lifted later and a pergola added to create a family sitting area when the children are older and no longer want to ride around this part of the garden on their bicycles.

The small store near the house is lockable and is a useful space to store both toys and garden tools when a quick tidy-up for guests is needed.

The swing and slide are easily seen from the house so that the adults can keep an eye on proceedings, while being far enough away to give the children a sense of freedom.

The stepping stones are set into the grass to make it easier to mow over them and offer access without treading on the grass too much when the weather is poor. The paths from the patio to the Wendy house are built from semicircular pavers, interlocked to give a hard surface that can be ridden on. The Wendy house itself is set in its own little area, surrounded by a green picket fence to give the children a sense of privacy without hiding it from view. The structure has been chosen so that in a few years, when the children have outgrown it, it can be turned into a very useful garden shed.

The play equipment is set on bark chippings, which provide a relatively safe surface and can be lifted easily when the play equipment is no longer needed so that the area can be turned into a border or put down to grass.

PRACTICALITY, VALUE FOR MONEY and safety are priorities in this garden, which is one in which children will play. It is important that children are safe and feel safe in their garden and that they learn to enjoy and respect their own environment. This garden is ideally suited to a family with children, and it is designed to make everyone feel welcome and to encourage the whole family to use it as a place to relax, play and enjoy themselves.

FEATURES

This garden has lots of features to interest children, and is safe and practical for them to play in. The built objects are robust, there are no hard corners, and lifted is plenty of room for games on the lawn . The fences provide privacy and security, while the plants and shrubs form an attractive surround.

The patio provides a hard area close to the house where children can ride their

The birdtable and birdbath will attract birds into the garden, and the children can help to put food out and keep them clean for the visiting wildlife.

PLANTING

The natural hedge at the bottom of the garden will change colours throughout the year, giving a sense of the change of seasons and lovely autumn tones.

Under the trees the grass is allowed to grow longer, with just a mown path running through it. The path goes nowhere, but it

creates the illusion that the garden continues, and it allows access without disturbing plants and wildlife.

Nothing gets children more interested in their environment than growing their own plants, getting grubby and generally doing all the things adults do. The children's garden is near the house so their efforts at growing plants will be readily seen by family and visitors, giving the children a sense of pride and achievement. Allowing children to have their own special area of garden limits the impact they might have on the rest of the garden, giving father a chance to grow plants, too. A bright kite mural is painted on the wall behind the garden, declaring it to be the children's own. Bulbs will appear each spring and the children could even sow wildflowers there if they liked.

A small collection of dwarf fruit trees will give the children lots of interest, and they can watch for the fruit growing and even help to harvest it. The tree seat will be a perfect place for picnics when the weather is warm.

The heather garden in the corner introduces a carpet of colour and a different level of ground cover.

opposite: A special area with a cheerful scarecrow, tall sunflowers and fast-maturing vegetables and flowers will give children a sense of achievement in growing their own plants.

above: Play equipment must be placed and secured on a safe surface and will give children hours of fun.

above right: *Helianthus annuus* (sunflowers) are quick growing and very impressive – in both their height and the size of their flowers, making them ideal annuals for children to grow.

TIPS FOR CHILDREN'S GARDENS

- Choose plants that are non-toxic and that will withstand the odd knock with toys
- Use a utility mix for the lawn so that it will take a fair amount of wear and tear
- Buy the best features you can afford so they last a long time
- Involve the children in every area they can safely take part in to encourage the next generation of gardening enthusiasts
- Grow easy-to-grow flowers, such as *Helianthus annuus* (sunflower) and *Lathyrus odoratus* (sweet pea), and lettuce and radish in the children's garden so that they get quick results and can take pride in their achievements
- Use good quality compost in the children's garden to give good results

WILDLIFE GARDEN

This integrated design offers a range of habitats to attract all kinds of wildlife, plus plenty of provision for the human visitors to the garden in a spacious seating area and simple wooden benches from which to view the animals, birds and insects that will make it their home.

PLANTING KEY

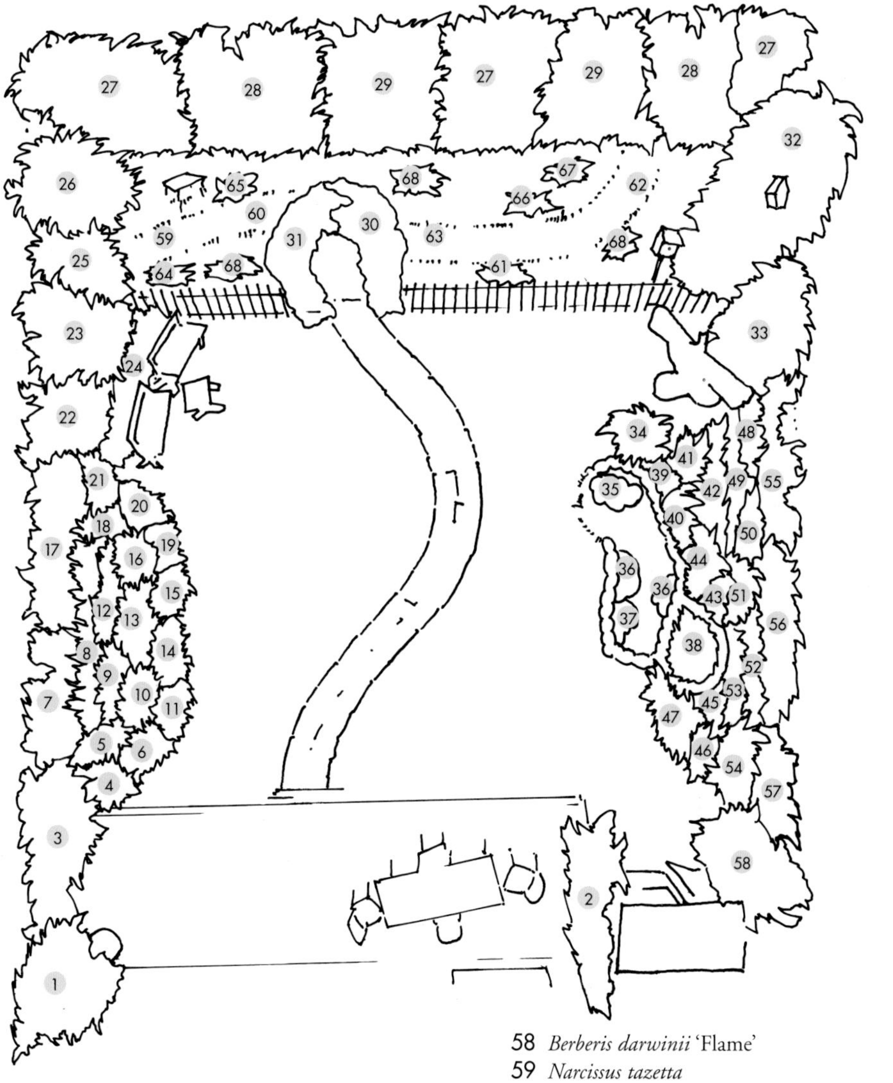

1 Ceanothus 'Cascade'
2 Lonicera japonica 'Halliana'
3 Actinidia kolomikta
4 Mentha suaveolens
5 Rosmarinus officinalis
6 Salvia officinalis
7 Lonicera fragrantissima
8 Digitalis purpurea
9 Calendula officinalis Art Shades Mixed
10 Eryngium alpinum 'Blue Star'
11 Allium schoenoprasum
12 Viburnum x burkwoodii
13 Veratrum album
14 Platycodon grandiflorus
15 Scabiosa caucasica
16 Lythrum salicaria
17 Campsis radicans
18 Onopordum acanthium
19 Nepeta sibirica 'Souvenir d'André Chaudron' (syn. N. 'Blue Beauty')
20 Lavandula angustifolia 'Munstead'
21 Tagetes Bonanza Series
22 Pyracantha angustifolia
23 Photinia x fraseri 'Rubens' (syn. P. glabra 'Rubens')
24 Lavandula stoechas subsp. pedunculata (syn. L. stoechas 'Papillon')
25 Symphoricarpos albus
26 Philadelphus coronarius
27 Fagus sylvatica
28 Ligustrum ovalifolium
29 Ilex aquifolium
30 Rosa 'Paul's Scarlet Climber'
31 Rosa 'Albertine'
32 Quercus coccinea
33 Buddleja davidii
34 Urtica dioica
35 Nymphaea odorata (syn. N. 'Odorata Alba')
36 Caltha palustris
37 Iris pseudacorus
38 Aponogeton distachyos
39 Mimulus cardinalis
40 Typha latifolia 'Variegata'
41 Lobelia cardinalis
42 Rodgersia aesculifolia
43 Osmunda regalis
44 Iris foetidissima
45 Veronica gentianoides
46 Primula florindae

47 Persicaria amplexicaulis (syn. Polygonum amplexicaule)
48 Hemerocallis citrina
49 Helleborus lividus
50 Euphorbia palustris
51 Digitalis ferruginea
52 Agapanthus campanulatus
53 Crocosmia masoniorum
54 Geranium platypetalum
55 Lonicera caprifolium 'Praecox'
56 Clematis macropetala
57 Rosa 'Chaplin's Pink Climber'

58 Berberis darwinii 'Flame'
59 Narcissus tazetta
60 Narcissus 'Peeping Tom'
61 Hyacinthoides hispanica
62 Crocus pulchellus
63 Crocus vernus 'Pickwick'
64 Anemone coronaria
65 Ornithogalum umbellatum
66 Leucojum aestivum 'Gravetye Giant'
67 Fritillaria meleagris
68 Wildflower mix

59–67 and 68 to be planted at random in the meadow area

THE VIBRANCY, COLOUR AND SERENITY of nature are brought closer to home in this clever design, which includes several different habitats within a single, fairly small site and provides opportunities for attracting a wide range of wildlife. The variety, scent and colour will please both the gardener and the wildlife. This serene garden is a haven that will hum with the activity of insects in summer and be a welcoming, restful place for you all year round.

FEATURES

The hard landscaping uses wood as the main material to soften the edges and allow nature to spill over into every area.

The main seating and entertaining area is a large expanse of timber decking near the house. There are several large wooden tubs filled with flowering plants, which can be changed seasonally. A spacious seating area in a natural material will limit the effect of the occupants on the rest of the garden and allow animals to come and go freely. A log path leads down the lawn towards an arch, which is covered with a tangle of climbing plants and through which the meadow area can be reached.

The raised bed, which contains plants that will attract bees, birds, butterflies and other insects, is edged with cut logs. This creates a change of level and brings the flowers to eye level. Two small trees back two simple wooden benches where you can sit quietly to relax and enjoy the rest of the garden. The pool is easily visible from here, so that you do not have to get so close that you disturb visiting wildlife.

Probably the single most effective way to increase the range and number of wildlife visitors to a garden is to introduce a pool and bog garden. The pool provides life-giving water, while the bog garden offers shelter and food in the form of slugs, snails and so on for the visitors to the pool. The pool does not have to be elaborate. Here, a small, natural-looking pool is set into a deep bed, the front of which is a boggy area, created by extending the pool liner into a shallow hollow. A tiny pool is provided for wildlife that does not like to venture far from the safety of the plants. Many animals, including toads, frogs, hedgehogs and voles, like having access to water but also will enjoy the proximity of the plant leaves and stems. The small beach area allows animals to drink safely from the pool without falling in and drowning as might happen with a steep-sided pool.

The stand of nettles will be a good place for several species of butterfly caterpillar, and the log pile will make an ideal home for hedgehogs, small rodents and perhaps even grass snakes.

PLANTING

Attracting wildlife means doing as little as possible to harm natural things by using chemicals, so companion planting is used to help control pests. *Tagetes* (marigold) attracts hoverflies, which will eat aphids, which may be partial to the tender shoots of the plants in the flowerbed. Some of the flowers are doubly fascinating – *Iris foetidissima*, for instance, has pretty flowers, and when they fade it produces pods that burst open to reveal bright red berries, which animals love.

Birds will be encouraged into the garden by the plants, but there are also two feeders to attract even more birds, which will eat a lot of the pests that can harm plants, such as slugs, snails and some insects. Having a wide range of wildlife in the garden helps enormously with pest control because, luckily for gardeners, most friendly animals live to eat those that gardeners find are a nuisance.

Beyond the arch is a meadow area, which is mown twice a year and planted with spring- and late summer-flowering wildflowers. These will attract many insects and small animals to feed on them and the grass seed. Two mown paths give access to this area.

The single *Quercus coccinea* (scarlet oak) will also attract wildlife. Most oaks can support more than 300 species of animals, birds and insects, making them the number one tree to plant. The batbox and birdbox should also attract residents that will further reduce the number of insect pests in the area.

The wide shrub border in the corner offers shelter and food for birds and gives a lush green backdrop. Climbing plants are encouraged to grow up the trellis, increasing the range of plants and the amount of greenery. Near the house *Berberis darwinii* 'Flame' will attract birds to its autumn berries, and the bird feeder will provide food for birds and maybe squirrels in the cold months.

TIPS FOR WILDLIFE GARDENS

- Choose plants that have berries or fruit for animals and birds
- Leave areas, such as the log pile and meadow, as undisturbed as possible to allow animals to feel secure
- Underplant beds and the meadow area with bulbs to give colour in late winter and spring
- Check and clean bird- and batboxes when they are unoccupied to prevent a build-up of pests
- Keep pools free of ice in winter so that there is always clean water available for birds
- Clothe the trellis in a mix of evergreens and flowering climbers to give variety throughout the year
- Choose plants that flower in succession around the pool to make it always attractive to insects

opposite: A mown grass path leads through a meadow rich in different species of wildflowers and grasses.

above left: A carefully positioned birdbox will attract nesting birds to the garden, although it may take a few years for them to decide to use it.

above: This attractive small pond, complete with waterfall, is surrounded by lush plants including large-leaved *Gunnera manicata*, feathery *Astilbe*, poppies and sedges.

FORMAL ROOF GARDEN

Pool, paving, pergola and planting - these four elements have been
used to change an unexciting corner of a roof into a pretty garden. Even the existing chimney
stack has been pressed into service.

PLANTING KEY

1   Wisteria sinensis 'Prolific'
2   Clematis 'Nelly Moser'
3   Lysimachia nummularia 'Aurea'
4   Hemerocallis 'Tobacco Road'
5   Heliotropium 'Marine'
6   Fuchsia 'Herald'
7   Solenostemon 'Royal Scot'
8   Solanum capsicastrum
9   Hypericum calycinum
10 Potentilla 'Etna'
11 Calamintha nepeta
12 Brunnera macrophylla
13 Phyllostachys nigra
14 Dicentra 'Adrian Bloom'
15 Gypsophila paniculata 'Compacta Plena'
16 Caryopteris x clandonensis
17 Lonicera periclymenum 'Serotina'
18 Phalaris arundinacea var. picta 'Feesey'
19 Cistus x pulverulentus 'Sunset' (syn. C. crispus
    'Sunset')
20 Hibiscus syriacus 'Woodbridge'
21 Buddleja davidii 'Empire Blue'
22 Luzula sylvatica 'Aurea'
23 Dianthus 'White Ladies'
24 Astilbe x crispa 'Perkeo'
25 Iris 'Gordon'
26 Hosta 'Yellow River'
27 Galega orientalis
28 Helenium 'Moerheim Beauty'
29 Dianthus 'Brympton Red'
30 Spartium junceum
31 Scabiosa graminifolia
32 Centaurea hypoleuca 'John Coutts'
33 Lavandula angustifolia
34 Rosa 'Cécile Brünner'
35 Nepeta racemosa 'Little Titch'

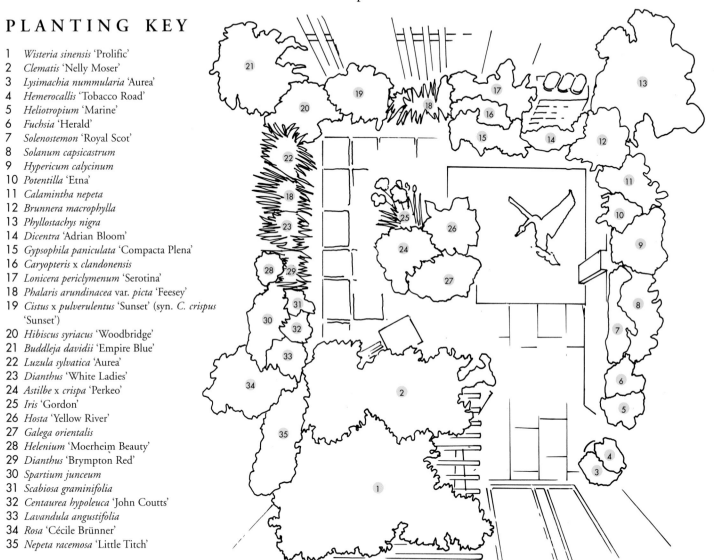

THIS FORMAL ROOF GARDEN elevates the gardener heavenward and makes the most of a small, sunny area. From being a potentially dull, overlooked and boring corner , the area has been turned into a beautiful and restful garden, far above the busy streets, where you can escape, entertain and relax.

Because of the sunny, light conditions, a roof garden is the ideal place for plants that might otherwise be difficult to grow. Once there is protection from the wind you can grow a far wider range of plants than you might imagine.

The important principals that apply to roof gardens can equally be applied to verandas and balconies.

FEATURES

One of the most important points to bear in mind when considering a roof garden is that the weight of the features, such as borders filled with moist compost and, as here, a small pool, will be enormous. Before embarking on such a garden, have a structural survey carried out. In this particular design, keeping the planting and structures near to the sides means that the most weight is as close to the weight-bearing structures of the building as possible, but a proper survey will identify any potential problems.

The materials used in this scheme link the house and garden so that the garden feels like an extension of the living area – which, of course, it is.

The uniform rectangular pavers are simple and with uncluttered lines. The planting is limited mostly to the raised beds, which are made from the same pavers as those used to cover the floor to avoid detracting from the spacious feel created by keeping the main area bare. Cleverly, the raised beds also form low walls along two sides of the garden, giv-

ing additional shelter and privacy. If your roof could not bear the weight of pavers, consider using artificial grass as a floor covering. It is much lighter and will add uniform colour.

The ingenious inclusion of the chimney-stack as a focal feature is a brilliant way of avoiding losing space by having to build a structure to hide it. In a limited space such as this, every feature, unless it is very unsightly, should be incorporated into the design. The chimney itself brings the raised beds nicely inwards to create a particularly stylish background to the pool.

A lot of space for plants has been created by using raised beds and slatted fencing. The wide-spaced slats allow light through while effectively enclosing the previously open side of the garden. The fence also hides an ugly view and defines the boundary, and it blends well with the mature brickwork of the chimney. The advantages of a slatted fence like this are that it provides privacy and offers some protection from the elements but it is not very heavy.

Shade is provided by a wooden pergola, made from wooden slats similar to the wood used for the fence, and this is covered with flowering climbers. The trellis on the wall and a planting hole make it possible to have climbers growing up and over the structure, making a private, shaded spot for sitting out. The simple furniture is wooden to bring more wood into the garden, reflecting the materials used for the fence and pergola and adding warmth and a natural feel.

The formal pool provides a large area of smooth water, which will mirror the sky and the clouds. Light playing on its surface will introduce movement, changes in colours and gentle noise. The elegant statue adds drama and style to the garden without dominating it. The choice of a bird has been carefully thought about, and it hints at a sense of freedom and power. The small fountain adds movement and will create ripples on the water's surface.

To extend the use of the roof garden, a lighting system could be installed. A small area like this would need a very simple system, but the effect would be instantaneous and you would have an extra room for much of the year. A light in the pool would also highlight the statue and bring the pool into relief during the hours of darkness. The interplay of light and water after dark is mesmerizing, and lighting would also, of course, make the roof garden a safer place at night.

An irrigation system could be used to make sure that the plants get adequate water and reduce the need for daily watering. Care should, however, be taken that excess water can drain away so that it does not seep through into the floors below.

PLANTING

Keeping the plants largely confined to the edges creates a sense of space in the centre, but the plants also play a part in providing protection from the elements and help to break up the potentially stark lines of the masonry. The diversity of the foliage provides the lush green normally provided by a lawn.

The largely evergreen shrubs will give year-round interest, and they are interspersed with a few fragrant plants that will flower over a long period and help to create a relaxed atmosphere.

Using plants that have slender, erect stems will add to the formal feel of this garden, and an unusual blue buddleia, *Buddleja davidii* 'Empire Blue', will look attractive in this setting. Plants that have grass-like foliage, such as *Luzula sylvatica* 'Aurea' and *Phalaris arundinacea* var. *picta* 'Feesey', will add to the visual impact and softly reflect the colours of the water and sky. Wind-tolerant plants will provide interest all year round and there are more plants than you might expect that will thrive in the sunny, windy conditions that are to be found on a roof.

opposite: A roof garden can include similar features and planting that is just as lavish as in a ground-level garden - provided due account is taken of the weight-bearing capabilities of the roof when working out the design.

above left: *Helenium* 'Moerheim Beauty' can be used to striking effect in a formal roof garden design if supported on boundary fencing or trellis.

above: Large containers on a roof garden, filled to overflowing with plants of all shapes and sizes, including climbers to make maximum use of the vertical space.

TIPS FOR FORMAL ROOF GARDENS

- Check that the structure of the building is strong enough to support your design and consider using lighter alternatives, such as artificial grass instead of pavers, plastic containers instead of terracotta, soil-less compost instead of loam
- Keep the central area clutter free and clean
- Use one or two strategically placed containers to draw the eye to special areas of the garden
- If wind is a problem cover the fence with netting, which will reduce wind flow

INFORMAL ROOF GARDEN

This small, dull roof has been transformed very easily into a delightful outdoor space by the addition of a bold chequerboard floor, pots of colourful flowers and a tree or two, preserving the beautiful view of woodland beyond.

PLANTING KEY

1　*Magnolia liliiflora* 'Nigra'
2　*Viburnum plicatum* 'Mariesii' (syn. *V. mariesii*)
3　*Begonia* 'Azotus'
4　*Tropaeolum majus* 'Tom Thumb'
5　*Pelargonium* 'Sandra Haynes'
6　*Hacquetia epipactis*
7　*Lysimachia nummularia* 'Aurea'
8　*Epimedium* x *rubrum*
9　*Pelargonium* 'Orange Appeal'
10　*Potentilla fruticosa* 'Golden Drop' (syn. *P. fruticosa* 'Farreri')
11　*Hedera helix* 'Goldchild' (syn. *H. helix* 'Gold Harald')
12　*Camellia* 'Royalty'
13　*Lavandula angustifolia* 'Twickel Purple'
14　*Tulipa* 'Apeldoorn'
15　*Hacquetia epipactis*
16　*Pelargonium* 'Rica'
17　*Hedera helix* 'Helena'
18　*Achimenes* 'Peach Blossom'
19　*Calceolaria integrifolia* 'Golden Bunch'
20　*Leucanthemum* x *superbum*
21　*Houttuynia cordata* 'Chameleon'
22　*Campanula carpatica* var. *turbinata*

23　*Hebe ochracea* 'James Stirling' (syn. *H.* 'James Stirling')
24　*Lithodora oleifolia* (syn. *Lithospermum oleifolium*)
25　*Vinca minor* 'Atropurpurea' (syn. *V. minor* 'Purpurea', *V. minor* 'Rubra')
26　*Fuchsia* 'Garden News'
27　*Peperomia caperata* 'Luna Red'
28　*Daphne laureola* subsp. *philippi*
29　*Salvia officinalis*
30　*Alchemilla mollis*
31　*Astrantia major*
32　*Spiraea japonica* 'Goldflame'
33　*Pelargonium* 'Spellbound'
34　*Petunia* Mirage Series 'Mirage Lavender'
35　*Glyceria maxima*
36　*Hakonechloa macra* 'Aureola'
37　*Crocus* x *luteus* 'Golden Yellow' (syn. *C.* 'Dutch Yellow')
38　*Begonia* 'Merry Christmas' (syn. *B.* 'Ruhrtal')
39　*Beta vulgaris* subsp. *cicla* 'Vulcan'
40　*Pentas* 'California Pink'
41　*Geranium sanguineum*
42　*Gerbera jamesonii*
43　*Griselinia littorialis* 'Dixon's Cream'

IMAGINE YOU ARE THE OWNER of a small area of dull grey concrete, shaded by surrounding trees and with low walls. The question is how to liven it up and yet not lose the interest of the trees and woodland beyond. The answer is to build a garden like this, which is made part of its surroundings by its clever design. What could be a dull concrete area is given character and life by bringing the surroundings closer, and it has been made fun by the checkerboard design of the floor, against which the plants and pots are brilliantly shown off. The plants are largely limited to the outer boundary so they do not compete with the strong statement of the floor. This garden is all about the interplay between elements within the garden and the wider environment. Simplicity and bold patterns make a powerful statement. This is an individual garden with lots of character, very carefully thought out and yet put together to appear relaxed and informal.

The garden is built on a roof space that is not constructed to hold a great deal of weight, so the plants are limited to the outer areas, close to the parapet, which is strong enough to bear their weight.

FEATURES

The strength of this simple and easily maintained design lies in the very bold black and white paving used to floor the area. Privacy and wind are not a problem in this sheltered site, so no additional structures are needed, apart from the urns. There are no plants in the centre of the area, partly because of the weight-bearing problem and partly because the flooring is sufficiently attractive to need no additional decoration. The parapet is high enough to provide shelter for the plants but low enough to permit views of the surrounding trees, and the planting around the edges takes the eye outwards, towards the canopy of the trees, and upwards to the sky.

No additional height is added to the parapet in the form of a trellis, for example, because there are no young children using this garden. The birdtable provides extra height and a link between the branches of the surrounding trees and the garden.

Casual furniture, in the form of a white lounger, chairs and a table, serves to emphasize the relaxed feel of this lightly shaded spot. The furniture harmonizes with the design of the floor, but does not draw attention away from it.

PLANTING

The containers used are all made of lightweight materials to avoid putting undue strain on the structure of the roof.

The lack of planting and variety of colour in the central area is more than compensated for by having lots of bright flowering plants in the containers. The troughs are set into the parapet, thereby putting additional weight only where there is already support.

The wall troughs are used to display colourful spring and summer flowers, and an informal effect is created by the random placing of containers to bring the planting gently towards the house. The two large urns on the corners of the parapet add height to the otherwise plain structure, and they draw the eye upwards. They can be planted with trailing evergreens or colourful flowers.

Plants have been chosen that enjoy semishaded conditions, and perennials like the trailing *Pelargonium* 'Orange Appeal' will

not only add bright colours to the wall but soften it with their tumbling foliage. Bright splashes of colour are provided by *Gerbera jamesonii* and *Begonia* 'Merry Christmas'.

The trees outside the garden are reflected in miniature within it by having two small trees, *Griselinia littoralis* 'Dixon's Cream' and *Magnolia liliiflora* 'Nigra', growing in containers, placed at opposite sides of the garden to reflect each other. The griselinia has beautiful green-gold leaves and makes a good windbreak.

TIPS FOR INFORMAL ROOF GARDENS

- Make sure that all urns and windowboxes are securely attached
- Use vermiculite or peat as lighter growing mediums
- Put large pots on wheeled castors so that they do not mark the surface and can be moved easily
- Intersperse the planting with splashes of bright colour so that the overall feel does not become formal
- Avoid structures that obscure views of the sky

opposite: The planting in the corner of this informal roof garden is kept below parapet level in order to make the most of the spectacular view.

above: The chequerboard floor is left clear in the centre, the containers of flowering plants being placed around the edges and on the parapet itself. Low planting ensures that any trees beyond the garden add interest.

CONTAINER GARDEN

The emphasis in this tiny backyard garden is on plants – lots of them, providing all the colour, texture and interest you could wish for without the use of fancy features and hard landscaping. The walls and floor have been kept deliberately simple, allowing the plants to do the talking.

PLANTING KEY

1 *Pelargonium* 'Voodoo'
2 *Narcissus* 'Tonga'
3 *Hedera helix* 'Cathedral Wall'
4 *Allamanda cathartica* 'Hendersonii'
5 *Myosotis sylvatica* Victoria Series 'Victoria Rose'
6 *Acaena microphylla* 'Kupferteppich' (syn. *A. microphylla* 'Copper Carpet')
7 *Zantedeschia aethiopica*
8 *Beaumontia grandiflora*
9 *Polystichum setiferum* Dahlem Group
10 *Origanum laevigatum* 'Hopleys'
11 *Allium* 'Globemaster'
12 *Oxalis enneaphylla* 'Rosea'
13 *Brachyscome aculeata*
14 *Papaver dubium*
15 *Osteospermum* 'Nairobi Purple'
16 *Hydrangea*
17 *Paphiopedilum bellatulum*
18 *Fuchsia magellanica* 'Versicolor' (syn. *F.* 'Versicolor')
19 *Anemone blanda* 'Charmer'
20 *Rhododendron* 'Anna Baldsiefen'
21 *Euonymus fortunei* 'Silver Queen'
22 *Oplismenus africanus*
23 *Nertera granadensis*
24 *Paeonia suffruticosa* 'Hana-kisoi'
25 *Onoclea sensibilis*
26 *Laurus azorica*
27 *Clematis* 'Horn of Plenty'
28 *Eremurus* 'Himrob'
29 *Allium schoenoprasum*
30 *Delphinium* 'Rosemary Brock'
31 *Artemisia ludoviciana* 'Valerie Finnis'
32 *Hedera canariensis* 'Gloire de Marengo'
33 *Erigeron* 'Dimity'
34 *Dryopteris filix-mas* 'Crispa'
35 *Hosta* 'Summer Fragrance'
36 *Geranium* x *riversleaianum* 'Mavis Simpson'
37 *Osmanthus heterophyllus* 'Aureomarginatus'
38 *Gentiana veitchiorum*
39 *Buxus sempervirens* 'Marginata' (syn. *B. sempervirens* 'Aurea Marginata')
40 *Parthenocissus tricuspidata* 'Lowii'
41 *Eriobotrya japonica*
42 *Buddleja davidii* 'White Profusion'
43 *Oenothera biennis*
44 *Bougainvillea* x *buttiana* 'Killie Campbell'
45 *Lupinus texensis*
46 *Melittis melissophyllum*

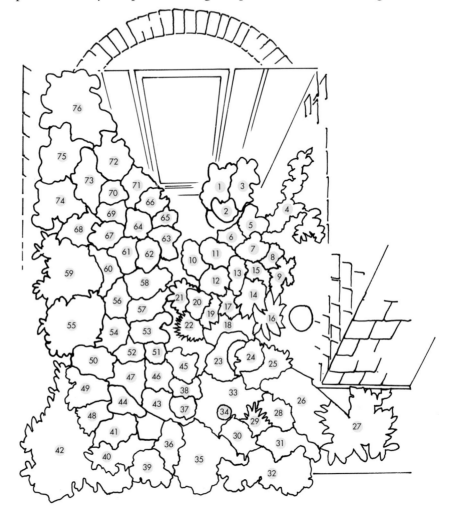

47 *Callisia fragrans* (syn. *Spironema fragrans*)
48 *Heuchera micrantha* var. *diversifolia* 'Palace Purple'
49 *Hemerocallis* 'Chorus Line'
50 *Filipendula ulmaria* 'Aurea'
51 *Calathea majestica* 'Roselinata'
52 *Euphorbia myrsinites*
53 *Clematis* 'Miss Bateman'
54 *Agapanthus* 'Dorothy Palmer'
55 *Pelargonium* 'Robe'
56 *Androsace pubescens*
57 *Astrantia major* 'Sunningdale Variegated'
58 *Armeria* 'Bee's Ruby'
59 *Aster lateriflorus* 'Horizontalis'
60 *Rosa* 'Little Buckaroo'
61 *Camellia japonica* 'Lady Loch'

62 *Begonia* Cocktail Series
63 *Diascia vigilis*
64 *Polystichum setiferum*
65 *Passiflora racemosa*
66 *Dorotheanthus bellidiformis* 'Magic Carpet'
67 *Chrysanthemum* 'Ringdove'
68 *Celastrus scandens*
69 *Rosa* 'Albertine'
70 *Hebe cupressoides* 'Boughton Dome'
71 *Alchemilla mollis*
72 *Alstroemeria* 'Ballerina'
73 *Artemisia* 'Powis Castle'
74 *Lonicera periclymenum* 'Graham Thomas'
75 *Hedera colchica* 'Dentata Variegata' (syn. *H. colchica* 'Dentata Aurea', *H. colchica* 'Variegata')
76 *Wisteria brachybotrys* 'Murasaki-kapitan'

FEATURES

The attention in this garden is definitely on the plants and not the walls or floor. These have been left bare and are not ornate or decorated. The floor area is covered with simple red, square pavers, which give a uniform base on which to build up the plants. The walls have been painted white to show off the plants and flowers and make the garden appear larger and more airy that it really is.

A small curved bench is tucked away in the corner farthest from the house, where the garden can be enjoyed to full advantage from a sheltered, shady spot. Apart from the bench, however, there are no structures in this garden, mainly because there is no room but also because everything you want, from shade to colour and movement, is provided by the plants themselves.

PLANTING

Container gardens offer endless opportunities to grow a large variety of plants because nearly all plants can, at some stage – or even for all of their lives – be grown in a container irrespective of their natural final size. In some cases, growing plants in containers will limit their spread and growth, making them suitable for use in a garden when, in nature, they would grow too large. *Ficus carica* (fig), for example, is a good container-grown plant that, if left to its own devices in the garden, can spread too much, as can rampant plants such as *Mentha* spp. (mint), which should be grown in containers so that you get the benefits of the plants but not their overwhelming effect on the rest of the garden. Herbaceous shrubs and trees are often grown in pots, but it is easy to grow fruit bushes and dwarf apple trees in containers, too, widening still further the types of plants that can be included in the scheme.

Containers can be bought in a range of materials, including plastic, terracotta, stone and lead, but you can paint and decorate them yourself if you want a particular colour theme. They can be stood individually or, as

WHAT WAS A RATHER DULL backyard has been transformed into a fragrant, colourful and continually inviting place, where you can sit in privacy and seclusion. Although it is small, the site has the enormous advantages of being fairly sunny and sheltered, making it possible to grow many plants that might not thrive in a more open, exposed site. If you find that one spot does not suit a particular plant, the container can easily be moved to another part of the garden until the right position for it is finally found.

Every possible space in this tiny garden is filled with colourful, fragrant plants. Containers, hanging baskets and tall wigwams have been used to provide different opportunities for plants to grow in or up, while trellis has been added to the wall to allow climbers and scrambling plants to cloak it in greenery and flowers.

here, in groups to make a display. Because you can move them around so easily, you can create different heights and shapes with the planting, a flexibility that is simply not possible with flowerbeds.

In this garden no single plant or feature dominates, and the eye is encouraged to range freely. This actually makes the garden appear larger as visual stimulus and excitement is provided everywhere you look.

Plants with unusual shapes have been used to add curves and interest. *Allium* 'Globemaster' produces smooth balls of purple colour, while *Zantedeschia aethiopica* has stunning spathes of pure white thrusting up from among the foliage. *Nertera granadensis* (bead plant), which does best in dappled shade, bears yellowish-green flowers, which are followed by masses of red shiny berries. *Hedera canariensis* 'Gloire de Marengo' has cream-edged leaves that add colour as well as evergreen leaf cover to a large wall or trellis.

Planting around the boundaries has been approached as if the garden were one deep flowerbed, with taller plants at the back and lower plants nearer the front. The difference is that plants here would not normally be found alongside each other. This is because every plant can be given a different type of soil, greatly increasing the range of plants it is possible to grow in a small area.

above: A tall, beautifully sculpted, urn is surrounded by a mass of containers, some hung from the wall, filled with plants grown for both flowers and foliage.

opposite: Bright red petunias are teamed with variegated ivy and other foliage plants in a contrasting rich blue container.

TIPS FOR CONTAINER GARDENS

- Make sure the soil in each container is right for the plant
- Mix commonly grown plants with unusual or visually stunning plants, such as *Zantedeschia* spp. (arum lily) and *Allium* spp.
- Keep a watch for pests such as vine weevils, which can spread quickly and destroy many plants
- Keep pavers clean and non-slip
- Add water-retaining granules and slow-release fertilizer pellets to the compost to keep plants in good condition

index

acknowledgements

Executive Editor: Julian Brown
Editorial Manager: Jane Birch
Senior Designer: Peter Burt
Designer: Les Needham
Picture Researcher: Zöe Holtermann
Production Controller: Ian Paton

Photograph acknowledgements in source order:

Edifice 73 right, 104.
Elizabeth Whiting Associates /Karl Dietrich-Buhler 76, /Andreas Von Einsiedel 6, /Jerry Harpur 56, 101 right, /Tom Leighton 84, /David Markson 11, /Michael Nicholson 13.
Garden Picture Library/Lynne Brotchie 21, /Linda Burgess 105, /Rex Butcher 49 left/John Glover 49 right, /Mayer/ Le Scanff 96, /Clay Perry 68, /Howard Rice 97 right. /JS Sira 89 right, /Ron Sutherland/ Chelsea Flower Show 1999 & design Geoffrey Whiten 'The Undivided Garden' 20.
John Glover 2, 33 left, 37 right, 40, 41, 52, 60, 65 left, /Design: Alan Titchmarsh 88 /Design: Mark Walker 22, /Design: Faith & Geoff Whiten 12.
Octopus Publishing Group Ltd. 93 right, /Steve Wooster 1, 109.
Harpur Garden Library 33 right, 37 left, 65 right, 69, 85 left, 101 left, /Design: Michael Balston, Wiltshire 72, /Design: Stephen Crsip, London 100, /Design: Gardening Angels 4-5, /Holker Hall, Cumbria 57, /Design: Gunilla Pickard, Essex 14, /Deisgn: Lisette Pleasance, London 77 left, /Design: Susan Rowley 108.
John Heseltine Archive 80.
Hugh Palmer 3, 18, /Design: Colin Livingstone 16, /Palacio Viana, Cordoba 77 right
The Interior Archive/Simon McBride/ Design: Jan Morgan 27, /Simon McBride/ Design: Simon Shires 26, /Ianthe Ruthven 44.
IPC Syndication/Nick Bailey 97 left, /David Giles 8, /Marianne Majerus 64.
Andrew Lawson 81 right, 85 right, /Bosvigo House, Cornwall 32.
Marianne Majerus/Design: Malcolm Hillier 10, /Design: Leslie Sayers 24, /Design: Thomasina Tarling 15.
S & O Mathews 53 left, 73 left, 81 left.
Clive Nichols Photography/Design: Mrs Preston 53 right.
Derek St Romaine 61 left, /Mr & Mrs Craig Eadie 36, /Mr & Mrs Foulsham, Vale End 61 right, /RHS Chelsea 1996, Sparsholt College, Hampshire 89 left, /RHS Hampton Court 1998, David Stevens 93 left, /Barbara Seagall, Holly Cottage 92.
Harry Smith Collection 48.
Nicola Stocken Tomkins 19, /Chelsea Flower Show 2000 23, /Design: Jane St John Wright 17, 25.
Jo Whitworth/Appletree House, Soberton, Hampshire 45.

Watercolour illustrations:
Trevor Lawrence 50, 66, 82, 90, 94.
Pamela Williams 30,34, 38,42, 46, 54, 58, 62, 70, 74, 78, 86, 98, 102, 106.

Planting diagrams:
Trevor Lawrence